European Computer Driving Licence, ECDL, International Computer Driving Licence, ICDL, e-Citizen and related logos are all registered Trade Marks of The European Computer Driving Licence Foundation Limited ("ECDL Foundation").

CiA Training Ltd is an entity independent of ECDL Foundation and is not associated with ECDL Foundation in any manner. This courseware may be used to assist candidates to prepare for the ECDL Foundation Certification Programme as titled on the courseware. Neither ECDL Foundation nor **CiA Training Ltd** warrants that the use of this courseware publication will ensure passing of the tests for that ECDL Foundation Certification Programme. This courseware publication has been independently reviewed and approved by ECDL Foundation as covering the learning objectives for the ECDL Foundation Certification Programme.

Confirmation of this approval can be obtained by reviewing the Partners Page in the About Us Section of the website www.ecdl.org

The material contained in this courseware publication has not been reviewed for technical accuracy and does not guarantee that candidates will pass the test for the ECDL Foundation Certification Programme. Any and all assessment items and/or performance-based exercises contained in this courseware relate solely to this publication and do not constitute or imply certification by ECDL Foundation in respect of the ECDL Foundation Certification Programme or any other ECDL Foundation test. Irrespective of how the material contained in this courseware is deployed, for example in a learning management system (LMS) or a customised interface, nothing should suggest to the candidate that this material constitutes certification or can lead to certification through any other process than official ECDL Foundation certification testing.

For details on sitting a test for an ECDL Foundation certification programme, please contact your country's designated National Licensee or visit the ECDL Foundation's website at www.ecdl.org.

Candidates using this courseware must be registered with the National Operator before undertaking a test for an ECDL Foundation Certification Programme. Without a valid registration, the test(s) cannot be undertaken and no certificate, nor any other form of recognition, can be given to a candidate. Registration should be undertaken

with your country's designated National Licensee at an Approved Test Centre.

Downloading the Data Files

The data associated with these exercises must be downloaded from our website. Go to: *www.ciatraining.co.uk/data*. Follow the on screen instructions to download the appropriate data files.

By default, the data files will be downloaded to **Documents\CIA DATA FILES\ECDL\ 5 Databases** (Note: *Windows XP* downloads to a **My Documents** folder).

If you prefer, the data can be supplied on CD at an additional cost. Contact the Sales team at *info@ciatraining.co.uk*.

Aims

To provide the student with an understanding of fundamental database concepts, practical experience in database design and implementation of the basic functions involved within databases. To familiarise the user with the main operating features of *Microsoft Access.*

Objectives

After completing the guide the user will be able to:

- Understand what a database is and how it is organised and operated
- Create a simple database and view the database content in various modes
- Create a table, define and modify fields and their properties; enter and edit data in a table
- Sort and filter a table or form; create, modify and run queries to retrieve specific information from a database
- Understand what a form is and create a form to enter, modify and delete records and data in records
- Create routine reports and prepare outputs ready for distribution.

Assessment of Knowledge

At the end of this guide is a section called the **Record of Achievement Matrix**. Before the guide is started it is recommended that the user completes the matrix to measure the level of current knowledge.

Tick boxes are provided for each feature. **1** is for no knowledge, **2** some knowledge and **3** is for competent.

After working through a section, complete the matrix for that section and only when competent in all areas move on to the next section.

Contents

SECTION 1 DATABASES..8

   1 - DATABASE PRINCIPLES..9

   2 - STARTING ACCESS..10

   3 - HELP..11

   4 - OPENING AN EXISTING DATABASE................................13

   5 - THE NAVIGATION PANE...15

   6 - THE RIBBON..17

   7 - CLOSING TABLES, DATABASES AND ACCESS....................19

   8 - REVISION...20

   9 - REVISION...21

SECTION 2 TABLES..22

   10 - MOVING USING THE MOUSE......................................23

   11 - MOVING USING THE KEYBOARD..................................25

   12 - CREATING A NEW DATABASE: DESIGNING AND PLANNING......27

   13 - CREATING A TABLE STRUCTURE..................................29

   14 - FORMAT FIELD PROPERTY..32

   15 - ENTERING DATA IN A TABLE.....................................34

   16 - DEFINING A PRIMARY KEY.......................................35

   17 - INDEXES..36

   18 - DUPLICATES..38

   19 - EDITING FIELD PROPERTIES.....................................39

   20 - VALIDATION RULES/TEXT..41

   21 - PREVIEWING AND PRINTING A TABLE..........................43

   22 - PRINTING FROM A TABLE..45

   23 - ADDING A NEW FIELD TO AN EXISTING TABLE................47

   24 - DELETING A TABLE...48

   25 - REVISION..49

   26 - REVISION..50

SECTION 3 TABLE RELATIONSHIPS...51

   27 - TABLE RELATIONSHIPS..52

   28 - APPLYING RELATIONSHIPS......................................54

   29 - REFERENTIAL INTEGRITY.......................................56

   30 - UPDATING AND DELETING RECORDS...........................57

   31 - REVISION..59

   32 - REVISION..60

SECTION 4 EDITING **61**

33 - CHANGING COLUMN WIDTHS 62

34 - FINDING SPECIFIC TEXT 63

35 - USING WILDCARDS 64

36 - EDITING DATA 66

37 - UNDO 67

38 - FURTHER EDITING 68

39 - ADDING/DELETING RECORDS 69

40 - EDITING SHORTCUTS 70

41 - REVISION 71

42 - REVISION 72

43 - REVISION 73

SECTION 5 SORTING AND FILTERING **74**

44 - SORTING RECORDS 75

45 - USING FILTERS 76

46 - FILTER BY FORM 77

47 - QUICK FILTERS 78

48 - REVISION 79

49 - REVISION 80

50 - REVISION 81

SECTION 6 QUERIES **82**

51 - QUERYING A TABLE 83

52 - SELECTING IN QUERIES 85

53 - SORTING QUERY RESULTS 86

54 - SAVING QUERY RESULTS 87

55 - PRINTING QUERY RESULTS 88

56 - QUERYING RELATED TABLES 89

57 - EDITING QUERIES 91

58 - RANGES OF VALUES AND WILDCARDS 92

59 - NON-MATCHES 94

60 - AND QUERIES 95

61 - OR QUERIES 96

62 - DELETING A QUERY 97

63 - REVISION 98

64 - REVISION 99

SECTION 7 FORMS **100**

   65 - FORMS 101

   66 - QUICK FORMS..102

   67 - FORM WIZARD..104

   68 - DESIGNING A FORM 106

   69 - EDITING FORM DESIGN..108

   70 - SORTING AND EDITING RECORDS 109

   71 - FILTERING IN A FORM 111

   72 - PRINTING FROM A FORM 112

   73 - DELETING A FORM...113

   74 - REVISION 114

   75 - REVISION 115

SECTION 8 REPORTS & EXPORTING DATA..**116**

   76 - QUICK REPORT 117

   77 - GROUPED REPORT: WIZARD...118

   78 - MODIFYING A REPORT 121

   79 - OTHER CALCULATIONS IN REPORTS 123

   80 - PRINTING FROM A REPORT...124

   81 - DELETING A REPORT..127

   82 - EXPORTING DATA...128

   83 - REVISION 130

   84 - REVISION 131

ANSWERS..**132**

GLOSSARY...**134**

INDEX..**135**

RECORD OF ACHIEVEMENT MATRIX **137**

Section 1
Databases

By the end of this Section you should be able to:

Start *Access*

Recognise the Screen Layout

Use the Ribbon and Quick Access Toolbar

Use Help and the Office Assistant

Open an Existing Database

Close a Table and Database

Exit *Access*

To gain an understanding of the above features, work through the **Driving Lessons** in this **Section**.

For each **Driving Lesson**, read the **Park and Read** instructions, without touching the keyboard, then work through the numbered steps of the **Manoeuvres** on the computer. Complete the **Revision Exercise(s)** at the end of the section to test your knowledge.

Driving Lesson 1 - Database Principles

🅿 Park and Read

A database is a structured collection of data stored in a computer system, such as a telephone directory, address book, etc. Each item of data, e.g. a single telephone number, may not mean anything in itself, but as part of a database, the data can provide information.

A database management system is a computer program that allows a user to create, maintain and process database files.

An *Access* database can consist of a number of related items.

All data in databases is held in the form of **Tables**, each table holding information on a single subject. Many tables may be linked together in a variety of ways to create larger and more powerful databases as the need arises.

Each line of a table represents a separate **RECORD**, consisting of items of data that belong together such as name, address and telephone number for a single individual.

Each item of data within a record is held in a separate column of the table, known as a **FIELD**. Different types of field can exist, e.g. text, number, date, etc.

Data can be presented in a **FORM** or a **REPORT**. Forms generally show one record from a table on the screen, usually in a neat and easy to read manner. Reports are usually presented so that they can be printed. They allow simple calculations to be made on the numerical data.

QUERIES allow questions to be asked of the data and display only the information required. Queries can include data from more than one related table and once saved, they can also be used as the basis of a form or a report.

Large scale databases are used by various organisations: by banks to keep records of accounts, by hospitals to keep patient details, by government departments e.g. the DVLA to keep records, and by airlines and travel agencies to maintain booking systems. These are just a few examples of where databases are used to manage large quantities of data.

Various types of people work with databases:

Database specialist/designer	designs and creates a database suited to the needs of an organisation.
Database administrator	controls the access to different data for specific users and recovers a database after major errors or "crashes".
Database user	enters and maintains (updates) data and retrieves information.

Driving Lesson 2 - Starting Access

▣ Park and Read

There are numerous ways to start the *Access* program. The following method is recommended for beginners.

☞ Manoeuvres

1. Starting your computer will automatically show the *Windows* **Desktop** with the **Taskbar** along the bottom. Click once on the **Start** button, , at the left of the **Taskbar** to show the **Start** menu.

2. Move the mouse pointer over **All Programs** to display a list of available programs, some of which may be included in **Folders**.

3. Click the **Microsoft Office** folder to display its contents.

4. Click **Microsoft Office Access 2007** to start the application.

ⓘ *Depending on previous use, an icon for Access,* 🔑 *may be found on the initial **Start** menu or even on the **Desktop**.*

5. The top line of the opening *Access* screen is the **Title Bar**. When a database is open, its name will be displayed here.

6. At the right of the **Title** bar are the usual **Window** control buttons, ▬ ▭ ✕, **Minimize**, **Restore Down** and **Close**. Click **Minimize**, ▬, to remove the *Access* window from the desktop. Click the **Microsoft Access** button on the **Taskbar** to restore it.

7. At the left of the **Title** bar is the **Office** button, 🔲. Click this button to show a list of basic database functions such as **Opening**, **Closing**, **Saving** and **Printing**.

8. There is also an 🔲 Access Options button here. Click this to display the **Access Options** dialog box. Settings can be changed here to control how *Access* will operate. For now click the **Cancel** button in the lower right corner to close the box and return to the main *Access* screen.

9. Next to the **Office** button is the **Quick Access Toolbar**, 🔲, which contains a few popular command buttons such as **Save** and **Undo**. This toolbar can be customised by adding further buttons.

Driving Lesson 3 - Help

Park and Read

Access has a comprehensive **Help** facility. This means that full advantage can be taken of the features incorporated in the program. Using **Help** can usually solve the majority of problems encountered.

Help topics are available either from **Microsoft Office Online** via the internet, or from the content installed on your computer (**Offline**). The method of using Help is the same in either case but the content may vary slightly and there will be some extra options when online. This guide assumes the **Online** option is selected.

Manoeuvres

1.   Click the **Help** button, 📖, in the upper right corner of the *Access* window to display the **Access Help** window. If the **Table of Contents** is not displayed on the left, click 📖.

ℹ️   *Pressing the <F1> key will display the same **Help** window. The window can be moved, resized or maximised if required.*

Driving Lesson 3 - Continued

2. **Help** can be used in two ways. Either type keywords into the **Search** box or browse through the listed topics.

3. Type **Printer** into the **Search** box and click, [🔍 Search ▾]. There may be many topics found for your search and it might be necessary to locate the most appropriate.

4. Click the topic **Set the default printer**. Help text for this topic is displayed.

5. Read the text then click the **Back** button, [←], on the dialog box toolbar to return to the previous screen.

6. Type **"delete a column"** into the **Search** box and click, [🔍 Search ▾]. The quotation marks force the whole phrase to be used and may help to narrow down the search.

7. Click the first topic in the list. Help text for this topic is displayed.

8. Read the text then click the **Home** button, [🏠], on the dialog box toolbar to return directly to the original help screen.

9. Type **xyz** into the **Search** box and click, [🔍 Search ▾]. Because the text is not found, some suggestions are made to help you find the required information. There are more options when connected online.

10. Click the **Home** button, [🏠], to return directly to the main help screen.

11. On the home screen all available help topics are grouped into a list of categories. The list is shown in the **Table of Contents** on the left and again in two columns in the main display area Click on the **Tables** category from either list. A list of topics under this heading is displayed. There are also two further subcategories which could be expanded.

12. Click the topic **Add or delete a column in a datasheet**. A substantial article on the subject is opened. There are many sub headings within the article and links to them are collected under the heading **What do you want to do?** Read some of the article. Use one of the links.

13. Click the **Home** button, [🏠].

[ℹ] *The **Table of Contents** can be hidden by clicking the [🔳] button.*

14. A button at the lower right of the window indicates whether you are **Connected to Office Online** or not (**Offline**). Click the button to see the available options. Click in the **Help** window to remove the options.

15. Close the **Help** window.

Driving Lesson 4 - Opening an Existing Database

Park and Read

A database consists of tables of data together with various other related items used for viewing and working with the data. Each table, form, report, query, etc., in a database is called an **object**.

Manoeuvres

1. Click the **Office** button in the top left corner of the *Access* screen and click **Open**, or use the key press <**Ctrl O**> to display the **Open** dialog box.

2. The default location for files is **Documents**. Double click the **CIA DATA FILES** folder, then the **ECDL** folder, then the **5 Databases** folder. A list of databases in the folder is now visible.

Open
« CIA DATA FILES ▸ ECDL ▸ 5 Databases ▾ 4ʸ Search
Organize ▾ Views ▾ New Folder
Favorite Links	**Name**	**Date modified**	**Type**
Recently Changed	Cia.accdb		
Documents	Daley.accdb		
Recent Places	Football Agent.accdb		
Desktop	Geography.accdb		
More »	Houses.accdb		
	Mailing.accdb		
Folders	Staff.accdb		
CIA DATA FILES			
ECDL			
2 Managing Files			
3 Word Processing			
4 Spreadsheets			
5 Databases			
6 Presentations			
File name:		▾ Microsoft Office Access (*.ac ▾
	Tools ▾	Open ▾ Cancel

> *If the data files have been stored elsewhere, select that location using the **Folders** list.*

Driving Lesson 4 - Continued

3. Click the file name **Geography** and then click **Open**. The **Geography** database is now open in the *Access* window.

> **i** *Opening Recent Database. A list of the databases that were most recently opened by Access are listed on the right of the menu shown when the Office button is clicked. Click on any of the listed databases to open it The same list of recently used databases is also shown on the right of the Access opening screen and can also be used to open databases when Access first starts.*

> **i** *The opening of databases can be controlled by adding password protection. If any database requires a password before it will open, the following dialog box will appear.*

> **i** *Passwords are case sensitive and must be entered in the dialog box exactly as set. None of the databases in this guide has a password, but be aware of their use.*

> **i** *In some networked systems, a Security Account Password is required before any databases can be opened. Contact your IT Administrator if this applies to you.*

Driving Lesson 5 - The Navigation Pane

▣ Park and Read

The starting point for many tasks in a database is the **Navigation Pane**, shown down the left side of the *Access* screen. From this pane it is possible to open, edit, rename or delete any of the objects (tables, forms, etc.) in the database.

The commands used to control *Access* functions are included in a **Ribbon** area along the top of the screen.

⟲ Manoeuvres

1. Look at the *Access* screen for the **Geography** database. The main structure is a **Ribbon** area across the top containing commands, the **Navigation Pane** down the left listing database objects, and an **Access Window** where the selected objects are created, displayed or edited.

Ribbon	
Navigation Pane	Access Window

2. Click in the top bar of the **Navigation Pane** to see how the objects are displayed.

3. The top part of the list shows in which categories the database objects are placed. At this level all objects will be grouped by **Object Type**, i.e. all tables will appear together, etc. This is the default setting.

4. The lower part of the list shows which categories of objects will be displayed. For large databases the list could be restricted to **Reports** only for example, but at this level all objects are required. Click on **All Access Objects** (even if it is already selected).

ⓘ *Make sure these options are set for every database that is opened in this guide.*

☞

Driving Lesson 5 - Continued

5. The **Navigation Pane** shows that there are two **Tables** in this database, called **Country** and **Regions**, and one **Form** called **Country Form**. Right click on the **Country** table to see a menu of options.

6. Click [🗄 Open] from the menu. This will open the **Country** table so that the data content can be seen in the **Access Window**.

7. Double click on the **Regions** table. This table is opened and displayed in the **Access Window** on top of the **Country** table.

8. Both tables are now open, and each open object has a document tab in the **Access Window**. The tab for the active or selected object has bold text on a coloured background.

9. Click on the tab for the **Country** table. The **Country** table becomes the active table with its contents displayed.

10. Right click on the **Country Form** in the **Navigation Pane** and click [📐 Design View] from the menu. The form is opened in **Design View** so that amendments could be made to its appearance or operation.

11. There are now three tabs in the **Access Window**. Click each tab in turn to display the three different objects.

12. Leave the three objects open in the **Access Window** for the next Driving Lesson.

Driving Lesson 6 - The Ribbon

▣ Park and Read

In previous versions of *Microsoft Office* applications, commands were controlled by a series of menus and toolbars. *Access 2007* has replaced these with a **Ribbon** which is displayed at the top of the application window. The **Ribbon** contains buttons and drop down lists to control the operation of *Access*. The **Ribbon** is divided into a series of **Tabs**, each one of which has a set of controls specific to a certain function or process. On each tab, the controls are further divided into separate **Groups** of connected functions.

Some tabs only appear when certain operations are active, for example open a **Report** in **Design** view and three **Report Design** tabs will appear.

☞ Manoeuvres

1. With the **Geography** database open from the previous exercise, click on the document tab for the **Country** table to select it.

2. On the **Ribbon**, the **Home** tab should be selected. Three other basic tabs, **Create**, **External Data** and **Database Tools** are available. One extra tab, **Datasheet**, is available because a **Table** is open in **Datasheet** view.

> **ℹ** *Any buttons displayed in pale grey are called ghosted and are not available to be selected at present.*

3. Notice how the buttons on the **Ribbon** are divided into **Groups** (**Views**, **Clipboard**, **Font**, etc.).

> **ℹ** *If the window is not maximised or the screen resolution is anything other than 1024 by 768, the Ribbon will not appear exactly as shown in this guide.*

4. Leave the cursor over any the buttons. A **ToolTip** appears which give more information and an alternative key press for the function if available.

   > Find (Ctrl+F)
   >
   > Find text in the document.

5. Some buttons produce immediate effects. Click the **New** button, 🖦 New , which is found in the **Records** group. The cursor moves to a blank new record at the end of the table.

Driving Lesson 6 - Continued

6. Buttons with a drop down arrow lead to further options. Click the **Go To** button, which is found in the **Find** group. A list of options is displayed.

7. Click the option. The cursor is moved to the first field in the first record.

8. Some buttons will display a dialog box which needs data to be entered. Click the **Find** button, which is found in the **Find** group. The **Find and Replace** dialog box is displayed. Click the **Cancel** button in the dialog box to remove it.

9. To create a new object, click the **Create** tab on the **Ribbon**. A new set of buttons is displayed, all concerned with creating new objects.

10. Move the cursor over the **Form Design** button to read the **ToolTip** then click the button. A blank form is displayed in **Design** view and two new relevant tabs **Design** and **Arrange**, appear on the **Ribbon**, replacing the **Datasheet** tab. One of these, the **Design** tab is automatically selected and contains buttons which will be used in creating a form.

11. Some buttons toggle effects on and off. Click the **Property Sheet** button, which is found in the **Tools** group on this tab. The **Property Sheet** panel is displayed on the right of the screen and the button is highlighted. Click the **Property Sheet** button again to remove the panel and the highlighting.

12. Click the drop down arrow on the **View** button at the left of the **Ribbon**. A list of the views available for the currently selected object is displayed.

13. Different views are used for different purposes. Select **Form View**. This view allows the form to be used for data entry or enquiry.

14. Display the other basic tabs, **Database Tools** and **External Data** to see which other commands are available.

15. Right click on any **Tab** name and select **Minimize the Ribbon**. The **Ribbon** is no longer displayed, only the **Tab** names.

16. Right click on a **Tab** name and select **Minimize the Ribbon** again. The **Ribbon** is restored. Leave the database open for the next Driving Lesson.

Driving Lesson 7 - Closing Tables, Databases and Access

Park and Read

Closing a table, or any other object, will remove it from the **Access Window**. If the format or design of any object has changed before it is closed, the message **Do you want to save changes to the layout...** will appear.

The whole database can also be closed. This process will first close down all objects which are still open, displaying the **Save** prompt if necessary.

*When a message appears asking to **Save**, it is always referring to the **format** of an object. Any data that is added to a database is automatically saved*

Manoeuvres

1. Select the **Home** tab on the **Ribbon** and click on the object tab for the **Country** table.

2. Move the cursor over the boundary between the **Country** column and the **Region** column. The cursor will change to ⊹ as shown below.

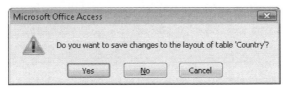

3. Click and drag to the right to enlarge the column. This is a change to the format of the table.

4. Right click on the tab for the **Country** table and click [≙ Close].

   > Microsoft Office Access
   >
   > ⚠ Do you want to save changes to the layout of table 'Country'?
   >
   > [Yes]   [No]   [Cancel]

5. Click **No**. The table is closed without saving the changes.

6. Right click on the tab for the **Regions** table and click [≙ Close].

7. Click the **Office** button 🔵 and select [Close Database]. The remaining objects are closed and the **Geography** database is closed.

8. Close *Access* using the **Close** button, ✕, at the top right of the **Title Bar**, or by using the key press **<Alt F4>**.

Driving Lesson 8 - Revision

This Driving Lesson covers the features introduced in this section. Try not to refer to the preceding Driving Lessons while completing it.

1.   Start *Access*.

2.   Open **Cia** database from the data folder, **5 Databases**, within **ECDL**.

3.   How many tables are in this database?

4.   Open the **Customer Details** table.

5.   Locate the **Copy** button on the **Home** tab of the **Ribbon** and use **ToolTips** to discover its description.

6.   Close the table and the database.

7.   Open the **Houses** database from the data folder. Right click on the **Location** table in the **Navigation** pane and select **Design View**. What **Tab** is displayed on the **Ribbon**?

8.   Close the database.

9.   Browse the list of **Help** categories to find a general article on creating tables in a database.

10.   Use the search facility in **Help** to find the same information by using the criteria **"create a table"**. Try and find exactly the same article as in the browse search.

11.   Close **Help**.

[i] *Answers to this revision exercise can be found at the end of this guide.*

If you experienced any difficulty completing the Revision, refer back to the Driving Lessons in this section, then re-do the revision.

Driving Lesson 9 - Revision

This Driving Lesson covers the features introduced in this section. Try not to refer to the preceding Driving Lessons while completing it.

1. Open the database **Mailing**.

2. How many objects are there in this database?

3. On which **Ribbon** tab would you find a button called **Run Macro**?

4. Open the **Mailing** table in **Datasheet** view. On which tab would you find buttons to change the font size of some text?

5. Start the **Microsoft Access Help** system.

6. Use the **Search** function to find information on "**Report Wizard**". Make sure you include the quotes around the text to search for the whole phrase.

7. How many results are found?

8. Within the results, open the topic that refers to grouped or summary reports.

9. Read the first page of this article then close **Help**.

10. Close **Mailing** database.

11. Close *Access*.

---

i   *Answers to this revision exercise can be found at the end of this guide.*

If you experienced any difficulty completing the Revision, refer back to the Driving Lessons in this section, then re-do the revision.

Once you are confident with the features, complete the Record of Achievement Matrix referring to the section at the end of the guide. Only when competent move on to the next Section.

Section 2
Tables

By the end of this Section you should be able to:

Use the Mouse and Keyboard to Move

Create a New Database & Table

Format and Edit Field Properties

Define a Primary Key

Create Index Fields

Enter Data in a Table

Create Validation Rules and Text

Print All and Parts of a Table

To gain an understanding of the above features, work through the **Driving Lessons** in this **Section**.

For each **Driving Lesson**, read the **Park and Read** instructions, without touching the keyboard, then work through the numbered steps of the **Manoeuvres** on the computer. Complete the **Revision Exercise(s)** at the end of the section to test your knowledge.

Driving Lesson 10 - Moving Using the Mouse

▣ Park and Read

To view more of a table, the **Scroll Bars** at the bottom and right edges of the screen can be used. To move quickly through the records, there are five **Navigation Buttons** at the bottom of the **Datasheet View**.

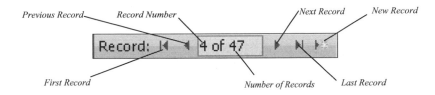

⌒ Manoeuvres

1.　Start *Access*. Open the **Geography** database, then the **Country** table.

2.　The table is shown in **Datasheet View**, that is all the information contained in the table is displayed in a grid.

ⓘ *Buttons at the right of the **Status Bar** allows the current view to be changed.*

3.　The table data is arranged in rows and columns. Each row **(Record)**, contains data about a specific country. Each column (**Field**) contains the same type of data, e.g. capital city or currency. The **Country** field is the first column, listing all the countries in the database.

4.　Move the mouse pointer over the middle of the **Region** field of **Brazil** (**South America**). The mouse pointer should be a I. Click the mouse.

5.　The cell will be highlighted to show it is the active cell and there will now be a flashing cursor within it. Using the mouse, click and drag part of the field contents. The letters will be highlighted when selected, ready to be edited if necessary.

6.　Click the **Previous record** button as shown, to move to the record above the current one.

Driving Lesson 10 - Continued

7. Record **5** is shown. Click the **Next record** button.

8. Record **6** is shown. Click the **Last record** button to move to the bottom of the table.

9. Record **47** is shown. Click the **First record** button to move to the top of the table.

10. Click the **Right** arrow in the horizontal scroll bar to scroll right by one column.

> ℹ️ *The horizontal scroll bar will only be present if the current table will not fit in the* ***Access Window***. *Reduce the width of the window if necessary to see the scroll bar. One way is to drag the right edge of the* ***Navigation Pane*** *to the right, making it wider. Don't forget to return it to its normal size afterwards.*

11. Click the **Left** arrow to view the first column again.

12. Use the **Up** and **Down** arrows on the vertical scroll bar to move up and down the table.

13. Move the mouse pointer to the left edge of the **Capital** field of **Australia**. The mouse pointer should change to ⊕ (this may take some practise).

South America	Buenos Aire:
Australasia	⊕Canberra
Europe	Vienna

14. Click the mouse. This will select the entire field.

15. Practise moving around the table using the various methods described.

16. Leave the table on screen for the next Driving Lesson.

Driving Lesson 11 - Moving Using the Keyboard

ⓟ Park and Read

The keyboard instead of the mouse may be used to move about the table. The following keys are used to move from field to field and record to record. Note that many of these movements only work when the entire field is selected.

→	moves one column to the right.
←	moves one column to the left.
↓	moves one record down.
↑	moves one record up.
Page Down key	moves one screen down.
Page Up key	moves one screen up.
End key	moves to end of record.
Home key	moves to start of record.
Tab key	moves one column to the right.
<Shift Tab> key	moves one column to the left.
<Ctrl Home> key	moves to the top left of the table.
<Ctrl End> key	moves to the bottom right of the table.

ⓘ *When two keys are mentioned such as **Ctrl** and **End**, the first key (Ctrl) should be held down while the other key (End) is pressed and released.*

Using the keys mentioned moves the cursor around the table by one whole record or field when the whole field is selected. Pressing <F2> toggles between having the whole field selected and having the cursor active within the field.

When the cursor is active within a field, some movement keys will move within the field content.

☞

Driving Lesson 11 - Continued

Manoeuvres

1. Click in the middle of **Brussels**, the capital field for record **5, Belgium**.

2. Press →. The cursor moves to the next character in the field.

3. Press **<F2>** to select the whole field then press → again. Now the next field to the right is selected.

4. Press **<Ctrl Home>** to move to the top of the table, first record, first field.

5. Press → to move to the next field, the **Region** field.

6. Keep pressing → to move right to the last field, **Language**. Press → again and the cursor moves to the first field on the next record.

7. Press the **<Page Down>** key to move down by one screen.

8. Press **<End>** to move to the end of a record.

9. Move to the top of the table by pressing **<Ctrl Home>**.

10. Press **<F2>**. The flashing cursor is now visible. The content of the cell could now be edited. Press **<F2>** again to select the field.

11. Click in the record number box of the navigation buttons and replace the entry with **22**.

Record: ◄ ◄ | 22 | ► ►| ►

12. Press **<Enter>**. The 22nd record (Italy) is selected.

13. Click in the **Search** field next to the navigation buttons and type in **Lisbon**.

Record: ◄ ◄ 22 of 47 ► ►| ►   No Filter   lisbon

14. The **Capital** field for record 37, **Portugal** is highlighted.

15. Click anywhere in the table and press **<F2>**. Practise moving about the table using the keyboard. Be careful, any changes to the data will be automatically saved.

16. Close the table and then the database <u>without</u> saving any layout changes, if prompted.

A common way of moving about in a table is to use the keys for moving from one record or field to the next and to use the mouse for moving from one area of the table to another.

Driving Lesson 12 - Creating a New Database: Designing and Planning

Park and Read

A well-designed database is the key to efficient management of information. Spending time at the design stage can save problems later. It is important to decide exactly what information is needed and how that information is to be used. It is a good idea to think "backwards" when designing databases, i.e. decide what information is needed from the database and then design the tables, etc. to achieve those aims.

The next step is to create a new blank database to contain the tables, forms, etc., that will be created later.

Manoeuvres

1. From the *Access* opening screen, click the **Blank Database** button to create a new blank database.

    Blank Database

2. This displays a new panel on the right of the screen.

    Blank Database

    Create a Microsoft Office Access database that does not contain any existing data or objects.

    File Name:

    Database1.accdb

    C:\Users\Brian\Documents\

    [Create]   [Cancel]

3. Use the button to browse for a location to put your database. Make sure the Folders pane is shown on the left of the dialog box. Click the **Browse Folders** button if necessary.

4. The contents of the **Documents** folder will probably be displayed on the right. Locate the data folder containing the supplied data for this guide by double clicking **CIA DATAFILES**, then **ECDL**, then **5 Databases**.

i *If your data files are stored in a different location, or you want to place your new databases somewhere else then this path will need to be changed.*

5. In the **File name** box, enter **Pets**.

Driving Lesson 12 - Continued

6.   Click [OK], then on the **Blank Database** panel, click [Create]. An empty **Pets** database is created in the folder.

7.   The *Access* **Database Window** is now visible with the database name in the **Title Bar** at the top.

8.   The opening view shows a new table (Table1) in **Datasheet** view. The table already contains one field named **ID**.

9.   The table could be used as the first table in this database, but the next Driving Lesson will demonstrate a more general method of adding new tables. First close the default table, **Table1** by right clicking on the **Table1** tab [Table1], and selecting **Close** from the shortcut menu.

10.   Leave the database open for the next exercise.

Driving Lesson 13 - Creating a Table Structure

▣ Park and Read

The table is the basic building block of a database. Every database must have at least one table. There may be many tables within a database, but each table should contain data related to a single subject, e.g. a products table, a customers table and an orders table. When designing a table **Field Names** and **Data Types** are created. These are the first things to be decided. Each field in a table should only contain a single element of data.

There are many different types of data that can be stored in an *Access* table. The commonly used ones are:

      Text   which allows text and numbers to be stored

      Number   which allows only numbers to be stored

      Date/Time stores date and time formats

      Currency   inserts a currency sign and decimal point.

      Yes/No   can only contain a **1** or a **0** but can be displayed as **True/False**, **On/Off** or **Yes/No**.

Creating the fields in a database table is an important process, as this defines what data is stored. Suppose a table of sales records is created that does not include a field for region. If six months later an analysis of sales by region is required, it will not be possible.

⌥ Manoeuvres

1.   On the new **Database** screen, display the **Create** tab and click the **Table Design** button.

2.   A new blank table (**Table1**) will be opened in **Design View**. This table will not be named until it is saved.

ℹ️   *Design View is the view that allows the structure of the table (or any other object) to be defined or amended. **Datasheet View** allows the actual data in a table to be seen and maintained.*

Driving Lesson 13 - Continued

3. This is where the **Field Names** are entered and where the type of data in the field is defined – **Data Type**. The cursor should be in the first row in the first column, under **Field Name**. In this position, type **Animal**. Press **<Tab>** to move to the next column.

4. The word **Text** appears in the **Data Type** column. A field with this **Data Type** will accept content of up to 255 characters or numbers. Press **<Tab>** to select the default setting of **Text**.

5. The cursor is now in the **Description** column, this column is optional. Enter the text **Type of animal** into this column and then press **<Tab>**.

6. The cursor is now in the next row down, in the **Field Name** column. Enter the words **Date Sold** for the new field and press **<Tab>**.

7. In the **Data Type** column, click the drop down button beside the word **Text**. A list of all possible data types is shown. Move the cursor over the **Date/Time** option.

Driving Lesson 13 - Continued

8.   Click to select this option, then press **<Tab>**.

9.   In the **Description** column enter **Date animal was sold** then press **<Tab>**.

10. In the next **Field Name**, type **Price <Tab>** and in **Data Type** select **Currency <Tab>**. The description is **Price of animal**. Press **<Tab>**.

11. The next **Field Name** is **Number Sold**, the **Data Type** is **Number** and the **Description** is **Number of animals sold**.

12. The last **Field Name** is **Delivery**, the **Data Type** is **Yes/No** and the **Description** is **Delivery charge?** This table structure is now complete.

Field Name	Data Type	Description
Animal	Text	Type of animal
Date Sold	Date/Time	Date animal was sold
Price	Currency	Price of animal
Number Sold	Number	Number of animals sold
Delivery	Yes/No	Delivery charge?

13. Right click on the **Table 1** tab and click [💾 Save] or use the key press **<Ctrl S>** to display the **Save As** message.

Save As
Table Name:
Table1
[OK] [Cancel]

14. Enter the **Table Name** as **Pet Details**, then click **OK**. A message appears regarding **Primary Keys**. These are dealt with at a later stage. For now, click **No** to save the table without a primary key.

15. On the **Design** tab, click the drop down arrow on the **View** button.

16. Click on **Datasheet View**. The table is now ready to accept data. This will be done at a later stage.

ℹ️ *Note that Datasheet View was the default view and could have been selected just by clicking the View button.*

17. Switch back to **Design View**, 🖉, for the next Driving Lesson.

Driving Lesson 14 - Format Field Property

Park and Read

When designing tables and applying a data type, the data being entered can be customised by having certain properties attributed to it, e.g. the length of text allowed, the date formatting, or the initial **Default Value**. **Field Properties** are applied in **Design View**.

Manoeuvres

1. The **Design View** of the **Pet Details** table should be open from the previous Driving Lesson, if not, open it.

2. Place the cursor in the **Field Name** column for the **Animal** row. The **Field Properties** will appear in the bottom left area of the window.

	Field Properties
General Lookup	
Field Size	255
Format	
Input Mask	
Caption	
Default Value	
Validation Rule	
Validation Text	
Required	No
Allow Zero Length	Yes
Indexed	No
Unicode Compression	Yes
IME Mode	No Control
IME Sentence Mode	None
Smart Tags	

3. Click in the **Field Size** property from the **General** tab. Helpful information is given on the right.

4. The field does not need to be so large. Delete the existing value with **<Backspace>**. Type in **20**. The field will now only allow 20 characters to be entered into it.

5. Click in the **Date Sold** field. The **Field Properties** are different for this type of field.

	Field Properties
General Lookup	
Format	
Input Mask	
Caption	
Default Value	
Validation Rule	
Validation Text	
Required	No
Indexed	No
IME Mode	No Control
IME Sentence Mode	None
Smart Tags	
Text Align	General
Show Date Picker	For dates

Driving Lesson 14 - Continued

6. Click in the **Format** property for this field. Drop down the arrow to reveal the choices for the date format. Click on **Medium Date**.

General	Lookup	
Format		▼
Input Mask	General Date	19/06/2007 17:34:23
Caption	Long Date	19 June 2007
Default Value	Medium Date	19-Jun-07
Validation Rule	Short Date	19/06/2007
Validation Text	Long Time	17:34:23
Required	Medium Time	05:34 PM
Indexed	Short Time	17:34
IME Mode	No Control	
IME Sentence Mode	None	
Smart Tags		

7. If a **Property Update Options Smart Tag** appears at this stage, ignore it. The format of the date in the table is as shown in the drop down list. No matter how the date is entered, i.e. 1/2/7 or 1 Feb 2007, it will be displayed as 01-Feb-07.

8. The **Price** field requires no changes. Click the **Number Sold** field. Use the **Field Size** drop down list to change the size to **Integer**.

General	Lookup	
Field Size	Long Integer	▼
Format	Byte	
Decimal Places	Integer	
Input Mask	Long Integer	
Caption	Single	
Default Value	Double	
Validation Rule	Replication ID	
Validation Text	Decimal	
Required	No	
Indexed	Yes (Duplicates OK)	
Smart Tags		
Text Align	General	

9. Click the **Format** drop down arrow. Look at the options available but leave the selection as **General Number**.

10. Click in the **Default Value** property and type **1**. This value will always appear by default in the **Number Sold** field when new records are added, although it can be easily overwritten.

11. Notice that *Access* has automatically defined this field as **Indexed**. This is not required. Cancel it by clicking the **Indexed** property and then use the drop down list to change the setting to **No**.

12. Save the changes to the table by right clicking on the **Pet Details** tab and clicking [🖫 Save] or by pressing <**Ctrl S**>. By default, the table is saved with the same name.

13. Use the [⊞] button on the **Design** tab to switch to **Database View**.

Driving Lesson 15 - Entering Data in a Table

Park and Read

Now that a table structure has been defined, the next stage is to add data to the table. Data is automatically saved as it is entered. Data can be easily entered in

Datasheet View (from **Design View** the **Datasheet** view button, [■], can be used to switch to **Datasheet View**).

Manoeuvres

1.   The **Pet Details** table should be open from the previous Driving Lesson.

2.   The empty table is visible. The field names are as defined in a previous Driving Lesson. The **Number Sold** field will have a default value of **1**, as defined by the **Field Properties**.

3.   In the **Animal** column, type the word **Dog** and press **<Enter>** to move to the next field.

4.   Enter the date it was sold as **24/2/07** and press **<Enter>**.

5.   Enter the price as **29.95** (do not enter any pound signs - this will be formatted automatically). Press **<Enter>**.

6.   Leave the number sold as **1** and press **<Enter>**. Click the box in **Delivery** to indicate **Yes** and press **<Enter>**. The cursor will now be in a position (under Dog) to enter the next line of data.

7.   Type the following data, exactly as displayed, into the table, remembering to press **<Enter>** after each entry. Make sure the **Number Sold** is changed from **1** to the value shown here. Leave the **Delivery** box blank to indicate **No**. Note that no matter how the data is entered it will be displayed as defined by the **Field Property**.

Animal	Date Sold	Price	Number Sold	Delivery
Toad	25/3/07	1.5	6	Y
Cat	9/4/07	17.95	2	N
Goldfish	1 May 07	2.25	11	N
Snail	22/6/07	1.1	34	Y

8.   Right click on the tab for the **Pets Details** table and click [Close].

There is no prompt to save, the data that was entered into the table is saved automatically.

9.   Click the **Office** button and select [Close Database] to close down the **Pets** database.

Driving Lesson 16 - Defining a Primary Key

▣ Park and Read

A database will often contain more than one table. In fact, it is desirable to have many small tables in a database rather than one large one, as this improves the efficiency of the database.

For these databases in particular, it is usual to use **Primary Key** fields. A primary key field is one that **uniquely** identifies each individual record in a table. This is often a number such as a serial number or ID number. Duplicate values are not allowed in a primary key field.

For those tables without a natural unique field (such as transaction records) it is common to add an extra field such as a sequential record number so that a **Primary Key** can be applied to it.

It is common to have the table records sorted on the **Primary Field**. This is done automatically. Using a primary key field allows tables to be linked together and also improves the efficiency of data retrieval and editing.

⌕ Manoeuvres

1.   Open the database **Daley** from the supplied data files.

2.   Right click the **Vehicles** table on the **Navigation Pane** and click to open the table in **Design View**.

3.   The field name **Reg No** should be highlighted. If not, click on it.

4.   Click the **Primary Key** button on the **Design** tab to make this field the **Primary Key**.

5.   Switch to **Datasheet View** using the **View** button. The following dialog box appears.

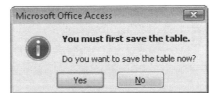

6.   Click **Yes** to save the table. The table will open with the records sorted in alphabetical order of **Reg No**.

7.   Close the table.

8.   Close the database.

Driving Lesson 17 - Indexes

🅿 Park and Read

An **index** is a copy of a field which is sorted and stored separately to speed up access to the data in a table. For example, to access a particular record in a telephone directory based on phone number, it would be necessary to search through the entire table looking for the number. If **Phone Number** was defined as an **Index** however, the number could be quickly found from the sorted list of numbers and this would link to the appropriate record in the table.

If a field is set as indexed, that table will be automatically sorted by that field whenever the table is opened. Indexing can be set on more than one field and the fields are sorted in turn. A **Primary Key** is automatically indexed.

👈 Manoeuvres

1. Open the database **Geography** and the **Regions** table in **Design View**.

2. Click in the **Region** field, then click in the **Indexed** field property. From the drop down list, select **Yes (Duplicates OK)**. Click the **Datasheet View** button and **Yes** to save the table.

General	Lookup	
Field Size	20	
Format		
Input Mask		
Caption		
Default Value		
Validation Rule		
Validation Text		
Required	No	
Allow Zero Length	No	
Indexed	Yes (Duplicates OK)	▾
Unicode Compression	No	
IME Mode	No Control	

3. The table will open with the data sorted in alphabetical order of **Region**. No other fields will be sorted.

4. Return to **Design View**, make sure the **Design** tab is displayed and click the **Indexes** button, to open the **Indexes** dialog box. The index created earlier is already shown.

5. Click in the **Field Name** box of the second row. Click the drop down arrow and select **Country** from the list. The **Sort Order** will default to **Ascending**. Leave the second row **Index Name** box empty.

Index Name	Field Name	Sort Order
Region	Region	Ascending
	Country ▾	Ascending

Index Properties

The name of the field to be indexed.

Driving Lesson 17 - Continued

6.   Close the **Indexes** dialog box and switch to **Datasheet View**. Click **Yes** to save the table.

7.   The table will open and this time the data will be sorted in order of **Country**, within the groups already sorted by **Region**.

Regions		
Region ▾	Country ▾	Capital ▾
Africa	Ethiopia	Addis Ababa
Africa	Kenya	Nairobi
Africa	Libya	Tripoli
Africa	Morocco	Rabat
Africa	South Africa	Pretoria
Asia	Afghanistan	Kabul
Asia	China	Beijing
Asia	India	New Delhi
Asia	Japan	Tokyo
Asia	Nepal	Katmandu
Asia	Russia	Moscow

8.   Return to **Design View** and open the **Indexes** dialog box.

9.   Position the mouse pointer on the **Selector Bar**, pointing to the row of the dialog box containing the **Index** name **Region**.

10.   Click and drag downwards to select the first and second rows.

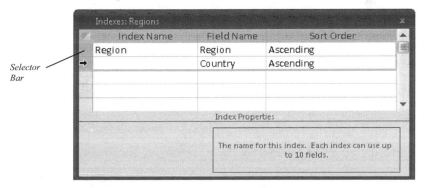

Index Name	Field Name	Sort Order
Region	Region	Ascending
	Country	Ascending

Index Properties

The name for this index. Each index can use up to 10 fields.

Selector Bar

11.   Press <**Delete**> to remove both the entries from the **Indexes** dialog box.

12.   Close the dialog box, click the **Datasheet View** button and click **Yes** to save the table.

13.   The table will open, with the data in its original order. Leave the database open for the next Driving Lesson.

Driving Lesson 18 - Duplicates

Park and Read

Indexes can be set up to prevent records being added with duplicate values in certain fields.

Manoeuvres

1. In the **Geography** database, open the **Regions** table in **Design View** and click in the **Country** field.

2. Change the **Indexed** field property to **Yes (No Duplicates)**. This prevents identical values from being entered in this field.

3. Save the table and switch to **Datasheet View**.

4. At the end of the table, click in the blank record in the **Country** field.

5. Type in **UK**. With the **No duplicates** index, if **UK** appears already in the field, then this second entry will not be allowed.

6. Click in the row below the new **UK** entry (as if the record had been completed). A dialog box appears warning of the duplication.

7. Click **OK**. Close the table. The dialog box appears again. Click **OK**.

8. This time a warning that this duplicate entry cannot be saved will appear.

9. Click **Yes** to close the object anyway.

10. Open the **Regions** table again and check that there is no duplicate entry – there are still only 47 records.

11. Close the table and the database.

Driving Lesson 19 - Editing Field Properties

🅿 Park and Read

Once **Field Properties** have been set in **Design View** for a table, they can still be edited if circumstances change or if it is realised that the full extent of the field will never be used. Unused areas make the database inefficient.

You may need to change properties for instance, if a **Product Code** field is set at **50** characters but the codes used are never more than six digits, or if it is decided that a different date format is required from that first used.

However, once a database is in use, consideration must be given to the consequences of changing any attribute in a table that already contains data. Changing a **Field size** from **30** to **20** characters will display a warning dialog box. If any actual data is lost by this change, it is lost permanently, it cannot be restored by enlarging the field later.

Changing data types in a table that already contains data can also have consequences. Changing a **Date/Time** field to a **Number** field will maintain all data but it will no longer appear in date format. Changing a **Number** field to a **Text** field will maintain all data but it will no longer be available for calculations. Changing a **Text** field to a **Number** field will permanently lose all non-numeric data from the field.

☞ Manoeuvres

1. Open the **Staff** database. Open the **Staff** table in **Design View**.

2. Click in the **Surname** field. It has a **Field Size** of **50**. Not many people have such a long Surname, so this may be altered.

3. Click in the **Field Size** property, delete the existing number and type in **20** – a more appropriate size.

ℹ️ *The default field size for newly created **Text** fields can be **255** characters.*

4. Similarly, change the size of the **Title** field to **5**, the **First Name** field to **15** and the **Position** field to **18**.

5. Click in the **Date of Employment** field. Drop down the **Format** options available and select **Short Date**. Do the same for the **Date of Birth** field. Remember, regardless of how the date is now entered it will appear in the table in this format.

6. Click in the **Salary** field. Drop down the **Format** list in **Field Properties**.

Driving Lesson 19 - Continued

General	Lookup	
Format		▼
Decimal Places	General Number	3456.789
Input Mask	Currency	£3,456.79
Caption	Euro	€3,456.79
Default Value	Fixed	3456.79
Validation Rule	Standard	3,456.79
Validation Text	Percent	123.00%
Required	Scientific	3.46E+03
	No	
Indexed	No	

7. Select **Currency** (note also that there is a **Euro** option). Decimal places are set to **Auto**. For currency *Access* assumes 2 decimal places.

8. Click on **Employee No** and then drop down the list in **Field Size** to see the various options available for number field size.

General	Lookup	
Field Size	Double	▼
Format	Byte	
Decimal Places	Integer	
Input Mask	Long Integer	
Caption	Single	
Default Value	Double	
Validation Rule	Replication ID	
Validation Text	Decimal	
Required	No	

9. Click away from the list to remove it then save the table. Because the size of some fields has been reduced, a warning dialog box appears.

> **Microsoft Office Access**   ✕
>
> ⚠ **Some data may be lost.**
>
> The setting for the FieldSize property of one or more fields has been changed to a shorter size. If data is lost, validation rules may be violated as a result.
> Do you want to continue anyway?
>
>   Yes   No

10. Click **Yes**, then switch to **Datasheet View**. Some data in the **Position** column has been truncated.

11. Switch back to **Design View**. Change the **Field Size** for the **Position** field to **20** characters.

12. Switch back to **Datasheet View**, saving when prompted. The truncated data has not reappeared even though there is sufficient space. Any data lost in this way <u>cannot</u> be retrieved.

13. Click at the end of the **Position** field for the first record and manually change the text to **Sales Representative**.

14. Similarly correct the other affected records (records **3** and **10**).

15. Leave the table open for the next Driving Lesson.

Driving Lesson 20 - Validation Rules/Text

▣ Park and Read

Validation Rules are used to set the requirements of the values that the user enters into a particular field. It defines the only permitted entries that the user may make.

If content is entered which breaks the validation rule, a message displaying some pre-set **Validation Text** will be displayed, as defined by the user.

Validation rules and text are defined in the **Field Properties** when viewing a table in **Design View**.

☞ Manoeuvres

1. The **Staff** table should still be open from the previous Driving Lesson. Switch to **Design View**.

2. Select the **Title** field and click in the **Validation Rule** field property. Enter the following text to define the permitted entries for this field:

   Mr or Mrs or Miss or Ms

3. In the **Validation Text** property, enter the following text as the message that will appear if any text is entered that does not match the list defined in the **Validation Rule**:

   The title must be one of the following: Mr, Mrs, Miss or Ms.

General	Lookup	
Format		
Input Mask		
Caption		
Default Value		
Validation Rule	"Mr" Or "Mrs" Or "Miss" Or "Ms"	
Validation Text	The title must be one of the following: Mr, Mrs, Miss, Ms.	
Required	No	
Allow Zero Length	No	
Indexed	No	
Unicode Compression	Yes	
IME Mode	No Control	

4. Save the table. As a new rule has been defined, the data that is currently in the table may not now be valid. The following message will appear:

Microsoft Office Access   ✕

⚠ **Data integrity rules have been changed; existing data may not be valid for the new rules.**

This process may take a long time. Do you want the existing data to be tested with the new rules?

[Yes]   [No]   [Cancel]

Driving Lesson 20 - Continued

5.   There are now 3 options. **Yes** will test the existing data with the new rule. **No** will not test the existing data but will apply the validation to all new records. **Cancel** will return to the **Design View**.

6.   Click **Yes** to apply the rule. All the existing data should already fit the rule.

7.   Start a new record. Enter an **Employee No** of **1050**. In the **Title** field enter **Dr**. Press **<Tab>**. The following message appears.

8.   Click **OK**.

9.   Enter your own title in the **Title** field (as long as it satisfies the rule). Press **<Tab>**. As it is included in the **Validation Rule** the entry will be allowed. Fill in the rest of the record with your own details.

10. Switch to **Design View**. Click in the **NI Number** field. In the **Validation Rule** for this field type in **Like "??######?"** where ? represents a letter and # represents a number.

11. The **Validation Text** should read:

   NI Number format is two letters, six numbers, single letter.

12. Numerical rules may be used. Set the **Validation Rule** for **Salary** as **>8000** and the **Validation Text** as **Salary must be more than the National Minimum Wage**.

13. Dates can also have validation rules applied. Click in the **Date of Employment** field and in **Validation Rule** enter **<=Now()**. This will ensure that the employment date must be today or earlier.

14. Make the **Validation Text - Check your date!**.

15. Save the table and switch to **Datasheet View**. The **Data Integrity** dialog box will appear, select **Yes**.

16. To test the rules, try to add the following record, changing to the alternative options on the second line when any value is rejected:

   987, Dr, Jones, Tom, MD, Tomorrow's date, M12345AJ, 6000, 2/05/60

   Mr   10/04/02   JM123456A 46000

17. Close the table and the database.

Driving Lesson 21 - Previewing and Printing a Table

🅿 Park and Read

Once a table has been formatted as required, it can easily be printed. A table may be previewed before printing to check its layout.

👈 Manoeuvres

1. Open the **Houses** database, open the **Houses** table and click the **Office** button.

2. Click the arrow to the right of the **Print** option, , and select **Print Preview** from the list of choices.

3. Positioning the cursor over the page changes it to ⊕. Position this cursor over the image of the data table. Click once to zoom in. The default zoom setting when zoomed in is **100%**.

4. The mouse pointer now changes to ⊖. Click in the page to zoom out. The default zoom setting when zoomed out is to fit a whole page into the window.

ℹ️ *The current zoom setting is shown at the right of the status bar along with a slider to vary the setting. Changing the zoom setting with this slider may affect the settings used by the ⊕ and ⊖ cursors.*

5. Zoom settings can also be changed from the **Ribbon**. Click the drop down arrow below the **Zoom** button. Try a few different settings then finally select **Fit to Window**.

Fit to Window
10%
25%
50%
75%
Zoom 100%
150%
200%
500%
Maximum 1000%

Driving Lesson 21 - Continued

6. Change the print preview display by clicking the **Two Pages** button from the **Zoom** group on the **Ribbon**.

7. Change the orientation of the print preview display by clicking the **Landscape** button from the **Page Layout** group on the **Ribbon**. This also sets the orientation that will be used when printing.

8. There are buttons on the Ribbon to change paper size and margins, or all settings can be changed from a dialog box. Click the **Page Setup** button then click the **Page** tab in the dialog box.

Page Setup dialog box showing:

Print Options | **Page**

Orientation
- ● Portrait
- ○ Landscape

Paper
- Size: A4
- Source: Automatically Select

Printer for Staff
- ● Default Printer
- ○ Use Specific Printer   Printer...

OK   Cancel

9. Click the drop down arrow on the **Size** field and select **A5**.

10. Change the **Size** setting back to **A4** then click **OK** to close the dialog box.

11. Click the **Print** button in the **Print** group on the **Print Preview** tab. A **Print** dialog box will be displayed. The options here are covered in the next Driving Lesson. Click **OK** to **Print**.

12. Use the **Portrait** button on the **Ribbon** to change the **Orientation**.

13. Click to close **Print Preview** mode and return to the normal view of the table.

14. Close the **Houses** table. If prompted, do not save the changes. Close the **Houses** database.

Driving Lesson 22 - Printing From a Table

▣ Park and Read

In a larger table, only part of it may be required as a hard copy. Once it has been previewed, perhaps only the data on the second page is required, or only the information in certain records. The required areas are defined in the **Print** dialog box.

☞ Manoeuvres

1. Open the **Geography** database and the **Country** table.

2. **Print Preview** the table, as described in the previous lesson.

3. Click the **More Pages** button, and select **Four Pages**.

4. Note the way the table is split over the pages. This would result in a very inconvenient printout. Select **Landscape** orientation. The manner in which the table is divided between the pages has improved.

5. Click the **Print** button on the **Print Preview** tab to display the **Print** dialog box.

6. Click the drop down arrow on the **Printer Name** box. All printers available from this computer will be listed. The printout could be sent to any of these printers by selecting it here.

7. Click the **Properties** button to see what features of the printer are controllable. Click **Cancel** to return to the **Print** dialog box.

Driving Lesson 22 - Continued

8.   In the **Print Range** area click in **Pages** and type **1** in the **From** box and **1** in the **To** box.

Print Range
○ A̲ll
● Pa̲ges   F̲rom: [1]   T̲o: [1]
○ Selected R̲ecord(s)

9.   Click **OK** to print page 1 only. Close **Print Preview**.

10. In the **Country** table, move the cursor over the first record (Afghanistan) and move it to the left of the table into the **Selector Bar**, until the cursor becomes ⬛.

11. Click and drag down all the countries beginning with **A**. They will now be highlighted.

Country ⌄	Region ⌄	Capital ⌄	Population ⌄	Area ⌄
Afghanistan	Asia	Kabul	14.8	0.25
Argentina	South America	Buenos Aires	31.9	1.1
Australia	Australasia	Canberra	16.4	2.9
Austria	Europe	Vienna	7.6	0.03
Belgium	Europe	Brussels	9.9	0.01

12. Click the **Office** button and select **Print**. From the **Print Range** area of the dialog box, click **Selected Records**.

Print Range
○ A̲ll
○ Pa̲ges   F̲rom: [   ]   T̲o: [   ]
● Selected R̲ecord(s)

13. Click **OK** to print only the **4** records.

14. Close the table and the database.

Driving Lesson 23 - Adding a New Field to an Existing Table

🅿 Park and Read

New fields can be added to a table, after data has been entered in other fields. Consideration must be given to data required in the new field for existing records.

👈 Manoeuvres

1. Open the **Houses** database and the **House details** table. It has been decided that a new field needs to be added to the table to record details of any offers made.

2. Switch to **Design View** and click in the **Status** field. The new field is to be entered before this one.

3. With the **Design** tab displayed, click the **Insert Rows** button, ⌐⌐ **Insert Rows** . The cursor is now in the **Field Name** of the new row.

4. Type in **Offer Value**, change the data type to **Currency** and the description to **Current highest offer**.

5. Save the changes and switch to **Datasheet** view. Note the new empty **Offer Value** field.

6. Find each record in the table with a status of **Under Offer** and add an **Offer Value** of a little less than the property asking price.

7. New fields can also be entered from **Datasheet** view. Click anywhere in the **Garage** column.

8. Select the **Datasheet** tab and click the **Insert Column** button, 🔲 Insert . A new empty column, **Field 1**, is created to the left of the **Garage** column.

9. Switch to **Design** view. A new field, **Field 1** has been added. Click in the **Field 1** row and click ⇒ Delete Rows .

> ⚠ **Microsoft Office Access** ⊠
>
> **Do you want to permanently delete the selected field(s) and all the data in the field(s)?**
>
> To permanently delete the field(s), click Yes.
>
> [Yes]   [No]

10. Click **Yes** in the confirmation box to remove the field.

11. Close the table, saving the changes when prompted, then close the database.

Driving Lesson 24 - Deleting a Table

P Park and Read

If a table is no longer required then it can be deleted. However, after answering **Yes** at the warning dialog box, this decision cannot be changed. The table is not sent to the **Recycle Bin**, but deleted immediately.

Manoeuvres

1. Open the database **Mailing**.

2. Right click the **Old Mail** table in the **Navigation** pane, but do not open it.

> | | |
> |---|---|
> | | Open |
> | | Design View |
> | | Import ▶ |
> | | Export ▶ |
> | | Collect and Update Data via E-mail |
> | | Rename |
> | | Hide in this Group |
> | | Delete |
> | | Cut |
> | | Copy |
> | | Paste |
> | | Linked Table Manager |
> | | Table Properties |

3. Select **Delete**. A warning dialog box appears.

> **Microsoft Office Access**
>
> ⚠ **Do you want to delete the table 'Old Mail'? Deleting this object will remove it from all groups.**
>
> For more information on how to prevent this message from displaying every time you delete an object, click Help.
>
> [Yes]   [No]   [Help]

4. Select **No** at this time to leave the table intact.

5. With the table still selected, locate the **Delete** button, ✕ Delete ▾, in the **Records** group of the **Home** tab.

6. Click on it. Again the warning dialog box appears.

7. Click **Yes**. The table is deleted.

8. Close the **Mailing** Database.

Driving Lesson 25 - Revision

This Driving Lesson covers the features introduced in this section. Try not to refer to the preceding Driving Lessons while completing it.

1.   Create a database named **Rivers**.

2.   Create a new table, and add fields as below with appropriate data types.

3.   Save the table as **Rivers** - do not set a **Primary Key** at this point.

4.   Enter data as shown below.

Continent	River	Length (kms)
Africa	Nile	6695
America	Amazon	6280
Asia	Yangtze	4990

5.   Switch to **Design** view and set an **Index** on **Length**, **Duplicates OK**, in **Ascending** order.

6.   Switch to **Datasheet** view and notice the changes in the order of the records, as indexed by length, shortest first.

7.   Add a validation rule to the Continent field, so that only the five main continents can be added: **Africa**, **America**, **Europe**, **Asia**, **Australasia**.

8.   Add validation text explaining the rule.

9.   Add 2 further records as follows:

    Mississippi   **It is 6270 kms long and is on the American Continent.**

    Zaire   **It is 4670 kms long and is on the African Continent.**

10.   Click the **Refresh** button, , on the **Home** tab to allow the index to reorder the records.

11.   Preview and print the table.

12.   Close the table and database.

If you experienced any difficulty completing the Revision, refer back to the Driving Lessons in this section, then re-do the revision.

Driving Lesson 26 - Revision

This Driving Lesson covers the features introduced in this section. Try not to refer to the preceding Driving Lessons while completing it.

1. Open the **Houses** database and the **Houses** table.

2. **Print Preview** the table and change the orientation to **Landscape**.

3. Print out only page **1**.

4. Close the table and the database.

5. Open the database **Cia** and the table **Customer Details** in **Design View**.

6. This table does not have a **Town** field in the address.

7. Insert a new field before **County** and call it **Town**. It is a **Text** data type and there should be **30** characters allowed.

8. Save the table and switch to **Datasheet View**.

9. Add data as follows:

Customer Ref	22	**Banbury**
	23	**Joincy**
	26	**Kirkley**
	28	**Braemoor**
	29	**Monmouth**
	31	**Keswick**

10. The following towns have been entered in the **County** field in error. Delete the data from the **County** field and enter it in the **Town** field.

Customer Ref	24	**Newcastle**
	25	**Boston**
	27	**London**
	30	**Derby**

11. **Towns** and **Counties** should appear as shown opposite. Close the table and the database.

Town	County
Banbury	Durham
Joincy	Durham
Newcastle	
Boston	
Kirkley	Durham
London	
Braemoor	Devon
Monmouth	Dyfed
Derby	
Keswick	Cumbria

If you experienced any difficulty completing the Revision, refer back to the Driving Lessons in this section, then re-do the revision.

Once you are confident with the features, complete the Record of Achievement Matrix referring to the section at the end of the guide. Only when competent move on to the next Section.

Section 3
Table Relationships

By the end of this Section you should be able to:

Understand and Apply Relationships

Create Various Types of Relationship

Delete Relationships

Apply Referential Integrity

Understand the Implications of Referential Integrity

To gain an understanding of the above features, work through the **Driving Lessons** in this **Section**.

For each **Driving Lesson**, read the **Park and Read** instructions, without touching the keyboard, then work through the numbered steps of the **Manoeuvres** on the computer. Complete the **Revision Exercise(s)** at the end of the section to test your knowledge.

Driving Lesson 27 - Table Relationships

▣ Park and Read

Tables in a database can be related so that data need not be repeated. For instance, imagine a Customer database with details of contacts, where many contacts are for the same company. It is not necessary to have the all the company details on each contact record. Contact details can be held in one table, including a single company name field for each contact. Using this field, the table is related to a Company table, where all the details for that company are held once only. This is known as a **One-To-Many** Relationship – one record in the first table (Company) can be related to many records in the second table (Contacts).

Tables are related using key fields in each table. In the first table, the key field will probably be the **Primary Key**. The matching field in the second table will have the same field name and is known as the **Foreign Key**, i.e. a unique field in the first table is matched with a field in another table.

⟲ Manoeuvres

1. Open the database **Staff**. There are two tables in this database that are linked by **Employee No**.

2. Select the **Database Tools** tab and click the **Relationships** button. The **Relationships** window is displayed. Both of the tables, **Staff** and **Courses**, displayed with a line joining the linked fields. The line displays a **1** and an ∞ showing that this is a **One-To-Many** relationship, i.e. one employee may be involved in many courses. In the **Staff** field list **Employee No** is shown with a key icon. This denotes that this field is the **Primary key**.

```
Relationships                                    _ □ X

    Staff                         Courses
  ⚷ Employee No        1          Date
    Title                  ∞       Employee No
    Surname                       Course
    First Name
    Position
    Date of Employment
    NI Number
    Salary
    Date of Birth
```

Driving Lesson 27 - Continued

3.   Notice on the **Courses** table that each record does not need to include all employee information, only the **Employee No**. This number links back to the relevant record on the **Staff** table, where all the necessary information can be found.

4.   Close the **Relationships** window.

5.   Open the **Staff** table. Remember the relationship between the **Staff** and **Courses** tables is **One-to-Many** (one staff member can have taken many courses).

6.   Notice that the table in the 'One' side of a **One-to-Many** relationship have an expand button ⊞ next to each record.

7.   Click on the expand button next to record 6 – Anthony Myers. The related data is from the **Courses** table is shown. This is called a **Subdatasheet**. This employee has taken two courses as shown.

⊞	517	Ms	Morris	Tracy	Telephone Sales
⊞	537	Miss	Lee	Ciara	Secretary
⊟	801	Mr	Myers	Anthony	PC Manager

	Date ▾	Course ▾
	25/02/1997	Virus Writers Workshop
	30/04/1990	Intro to Access
✱		

⊞	895	Mr	Valdron	Brian	Programmer
⊞	900	Mrs	Jones	Lesley	Admin Assistant
⊞	921	Ms	Parr	Norma	Foreman

8.   Click on the minus sign (collapse button) to close the related table, then view the **Subdatasheet** for other related records.

9.   Close the table and the database.

Driving Lesson 28 - Applying Relationships

🅿 Park and Read

Once tables have been designed and primary keys applied, a **Relationship** may be applied between two or more tables to link them together.

Relationships are applied between tables that contain a common field. Usually, the related field in one table is the primary key field and so this table is the **Primary Table**.

Applying relationships allows many smaller tables to be linked together to form the complete database, improving its overall efficiency.

Manoeuvres

1. Open the database **Daley**.

2. Click the **Relationships** button, found on the **Database Tools** tab. The **Relationships** window will be empty as there are no relationships currently defined.

3. If the **Show Table** dialog box does not appear, click the **Show Table** button, on the **Design** tab.

> ℹ Alternatively right click the **Relationship** window and select **Show Table** from the shortcut menu.

4. With the **Tables** tab selected, click on **Vehicles** to highlight it, then click **Add** to place that table in the **Relationships** window.

Driving Lesson 28 - Continued

5.　　Click the **Repairs** table and add it to the window.

6.　　Click [**Close**] to remove the **Show Table** dialog box.

7.　　Click and drag the table edges to resize the table boxes to be able to see all of their fields. Notice the **Primary Keys** for each table are indicated by the key icon.

8.　　Highlight the **Reg No** field in the **Vehicles** table.

9.　　Drag the **Reg No** field, from the **Vehicles** table, over the **Reg No** field in the **Repairs** table. Release the mouse when in position.

10.　In the **Edit Relationships** dialog box, note the relationship type is **One-To-Many**. This is because **Reg No** is the primary key in the first table but is just a normal non-unique field in the second table.

11.　Click [**Create**] to create the relationship then leave the database open for the next exercise.

Driving Lesson 29 - Referential Integrity

🅿 Park and Read

Referential Integrity is a set of rules which can be applied to relationships, ensuring they are valid and that data is not accidentally deleted or changed. It may be applied when specific conditions are met: the matching field from the primary table is a primary key, the related fields are the same data types and both tables belong to the same database.

Enforcing referential integrity does not allow the primary key data in the primary table to be changed, nor does it allow deletion of any record from the primary table, if a related record exists elsewhere. A record cannot be added to a related table if a record does not exist in the primary table, e.g. there can be no job record without an associated car record in the primary table.

🖙 Manoeuvres

1. Make sure the **Relationships** display for the **Daley** database is still open.

2. Right click with the mouse on the relationship line between **Vehicles** and **Repairs** and select **Edit Relationship** from the menu.

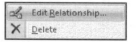

3. In the **Edit Relationship** dialog box, check the box for **Enforce Referential Integrity** and click ⬚ OK ⬚.

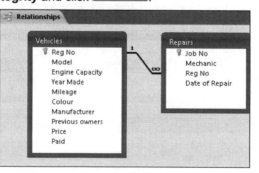

ℹ️ *Enforcing Referential Integrity will change the relationship line to show the type of relationship, in this case, one to many.*

4. Close the **Relationship** window, selecting **Yes** if prompted to save. Leave the database open for the next exercise.

Driving Lesson 30 - Updating and Deleting Records

▣ Park and Read

If referential integrity is enforced, the deletion of records from the primary table is controlled as is the updating of primary key data. Similarly a related record in a table may not be created, if a field is not available in the primary table.

☞ Manoeuvres

1. Open the **Vehicles** table in **Datasheet View**.

2. Click to the left of the record **R654 TFG** to select the entire record and click the **Delete Record** button, ✕ Delete ▾, on the **Home** tab. The record may not be deleted, as there are records in the **Repairs** table that refer back to this record, i.e. repairs for vehicle **R654 TFG**.

> Microsoft Office Access
>
> ⚠ The record cannot be deleted or changed because table 'Repairs' includes related records.
>
> [OK]   [Help]

3. Click **OK**. Close the table.

4. Open the **Repairs** table in **Datasheet View**.

5. On the **Home** tab, click the **New Record** button, ▭ New in the **Records** group and create a new record by typing in the following data:
    David   E789 ABC   5/1/2

ℹ *The **Job No** cannot be entered, it is an **AutoNumber** field that is filled in automatically.*

6. Press **<Enter>** after the last entry. As there is no registration number for this job in the **Vehicles** table, a new job record cannot be created.

> Microsoft Office Access
>
> ⚠ You cannot add or change a record because a related record is required in table 'Vehicles'.
>
> [OK]   [Help]

7. Click **OK**. Delete the information just entered using **Undo**. Close the table.

Driving Lesson 30 - Continued

8. To allow editing or deletion of records, the relationship between the tables must be changed. Click the **Relationships** button.

9. Right click on the linking line between **Vehicles** and **Repairs** and select **Edit Relationship**.

10. Edit the relationship as follows: check the boxes for **Cascade Update Related Fields** and **Cascade Delete Related Records**. This means that any changes made in one related table will be reflected in the others.

11. Click **OK**.

12. Close the **Relationships** window, saving the **Relationship**, if prompted.

13. Open the **Vehicles** table in **Datasheet View** and delete the record for the **Quattro, 379 CZ**.

14. The dialog box is a warning that there are records in other tables for this vehicle and they too will be deleted. Read the dialog box then select **Yes**.

15. Change the registration **E666 RPR** to **E666 RPQ**.

16. Close the table and open the **Repairs** table in **Datasheet View**. All jobs for the Quattro are removed (**Job 11**) and the registration number change has been reflected in the **Repairs** table (**Job 13**).

17. Close the table and the database.

Driving Lesson 31 - Revision

This Driving Lesson covers the features introduced in this section. Try not to refer to the preceding Driving Lessons while completing it.

1.　Open the database **Football Agent**.

2.　Open the **Current Status** table to view the information available to the Agent. Close the table.

3.　Open the **Relationships** window and establish a relationship between the **Current Status** table and **Past Clubs** using the **Ref Code**.

4.　Enforce **Referential Integrity** and **Cascade** all information.

5.　Open the **Current Status** table and view the data.

6.　Use the subdatasheets to view the related data from the **Past Clubs** table. Do not make any changes.

7.　Close the table and the database.

If you experienced any difficulty completing the Revision, refer back to the Driving Lessons in this section, then re-do the revision.

Driving Lesson 32 - Revision

This Driving Lesson covers the features introduced in this section. Try not to refer to the preceding Driving Lessons while completing it.

1. Open the **Cia** database and view the tables that are available. This is a typical database used by a retailer to keep track of customers and suppliers.

2. Open the **Suppliers** table in **Datasheet View**. Notice that there is no way from this table to see which products are supplied by each supplier.

3. Open the **Relationships** window and establish the following **One-to-Many** relationships, enforcing referential integrity and cascading all information.

    Customer Details table – Orders table by Customer Ref

    Orders table – Order Details table by Order Ref

    Order Details table – Products table by Product Ref

    Products table – Suppliers table by Supplier Ref

4. Close the **Relationships** window and open the **Customer Details** table. View the data and the related data through the several layers of subdatasheets.

[i] *Subdatasheets are only shown for relationships when the direction is one to many, not many to one.*

5. Close the table.

6. Open the **Suppliers** table in **Datasheet View**. Use subdatasheets to see which products they supply.

7. Close the **Relationships** window and the database.

If you experienced any difficulty completing the Revision, refer back to the Driving Lessons in this section, then re-do the revision.

Once you are confident with the features, complete the Record of Achievement Matrix referring to the section at the end of the guide. Only when competent move on to the next Section.

Section 4
Editing

By the end of the Section you should be able to:

Change Column Width

Find Text

Edit and Delete Data

Use Undo

Add & Delete Records

Use Wildcards to Search

Edit and Enter Data using Shortcuts

To gain an understanding of the above features, work through the **Driving Lessons** in this **Section**.

For each **Driving Lesson**, read the **Park and Read** instructions, without touching the keyboard, then work through the numbered steps of the **Manoeuvres** on the computer. Complete the **Revision Exercise(s)** at the end of the section to test your knowledge.

Driving Lesson 33 - Changing Column Widths

▣ Park and Read

Column Widths can be changed to allow data to be read more easily. The width of the columns can be set using the menus or the mouse.

⟨ᐟ⟩ Manoeuvres

1.   Open the **Houses** database and the table **Houses** within it.

2.   Right click in the column heading for the **Town** column. A shortcut menu of column functions is displayed. Select **Column Width**.

3.   Enter **10** in the **Column Width** box. Click **OK**. The column is now narrower. The data is still there, it just cannot be fully seen.

4.   Move the mouse pointer into the column border between the **Address** and the **Type** field headings. The pointer will change to a ✛.

5.   Click and drag the column border to the left, until the **Address** field is about half its present width, then release the mouse button.

6.   Position the mouse pointer on the column border between the **Address** and the **Type** fields again and double click the mouse button. The column will automatically adjust to fit the widest entry.

7.   Select the first 4 columns by clicking and dragging the first four column headers. Right click in the headers and select **Column Width**.

ℹ️ *Do not start the click and drag on a column that is already selected or the column will be moved.*

8.   Enter **15** into the **Column Width** box then click **OK**. All 4 columns are now the same size.

9.   Select all the columns in the table. Double click any header border or right click in the headers, select **Column Width** then click **Best Fit**. All columns are resized.

10.   Close the table. As design changes have been made, you will be prompted to save the changes. Select **Yes**.

11.   Close the database.

Driving Lesson 34 - Finding Specific Text

▣ Park and Read

Access will search a table for specific information based on given criteria using **Find**. Once the text has been specified, *Access* will search the table for the value. The search can be restricted to a single field only. The search starts at the cursor position.

♞ Manoeuvres

1.   Open the **Staff** database. Open the table **Staff**.

2.   Click in the **First Name** field of the first record then click the **Find** button on the **Ribbon**.

3.   In the **Find What** field type **Anthony**. Make sure the other settings are as shown below.

Find and Replace
Find   Replace
Find What: Anthony   ▾   [Find Next]
[Cancel]
Look In: First Name ▾
Match: Whole Field ▾
Search: All ▾
☐ Match Case   ☑ Search Fields As Formatted

4.   Click the **Find Next** button. The message **Search succeeded** appears in the **Status Bar** and current record is now **Record 6**.

ℹ️   *If the **Find and Replace** dialog box is obstructing the view of the table, position the mouse pointer over the **Title Bar** and click and drag to a new position.*

5.   Click **Find Next** to jump to the next occurrence of **Anthony**. The current record is now **Record 10**.

6.   Select **Find Next** again. The end of search message appears.

7.   Select **OK** and then click the **Cancel** button to close the **Find and Replace** dialog box.

8.   In the **Date of Employment** field search for **01/12/1986** and note the record number. (If unsure of how the field is formatted, uncheck **Search Fields As Formatted**, and any date format will be found, e.g. 1/12/86).

9.   In the **Employee No** field, search for **900**. What is its record number?

10.   Close the table and then close the database.

ℹ️   *Answers to this exercise can be found at the end of this guide.*

Driving Lesson 35 - Using Wildcards

▣ Park and Read

There are three **Wildcards** that can be used to help find matching text in a table. The wildcards replace either one letter or a group of letters when entering the required text. They are used when the exact form of the text is not known.

?	represents a **single** alphabetic character.
#	represents a **single** numeric character
***	represents any **group** of characters.
e.g.	To search for Smith or Smyth, enter **Sm?th**.
	To search for Chapman or Coleman, enter **C*man**.

ℝ Manoeuvres

1. Open the database **Geography** and then open the **Country** table.

2. Move the cursor into the first record of the **Capital** field and click the **Find** button.

3. The text to search for will be **Tok?o**, not knowing whether the spelling is Tokio or Tokyo. In the **Find What** box enter **Tok?o**.

4. Click the **Find Next** button. When the message **Search succeeded** appears in the **Status Bar**, select **Cancel** to close the **Find and Replace** dialog box and see the position of the cursor. Record **23** and the field containing **Tokyo** will be highlighted.

5. Place the cursor in the **Currency** field and select the **Find** button.

6. In the **Find What** box, enter **D*r**. This search will find all currencies beginning with a **D** and ending in an **r**, with any text in between.

7. Use the **Find Next** button to jump through the records as necessary. Select **OK** at the end of the search and **Cancel** to discontinue searching. There are **7** matches.

8. Search the whole table for any word or multiple words that begins with a G and has an E in it. To search the whole table rather than a specific column, click the drop down arrow in the **Look In** box and select the table name, **Country**, from the list. Use **g*e*** in the **Find What** box.

Driving Lesson 35 - Continued

```
Find and Replace                                              ? ☒
 ┌──────┬─────────┐
 │ Find │ Replace │
 └──────┴─────────┘
  Find What:    g*e*                                   ▼    [ Find Next ]

                                                            [  Cancel  ]

  Look In:      Country  ▼
  Match:        Whole Field  ▼
  Search:       All  ▼
                ☐ Match Case   ☑ Search Fields As Formatted
```

9. Find all the matches – there should be matches for Germany, German(3), Greece and Greek, **6** in total.

10. Find which countries are in a **Region** that includes the word **America**. Click in the **Region** column, select **Region** in the **Look In** box, enter **america** in the **Find What** box and select **Any Part of Field** in the **Match** box.

11. Find the matches then close the **Find and Replace** box.

12. Position the cursor in the **Population** field. Click the **Find** button.

13. Change the value in **Match** back to **Whole Field**. Type **4.#** in **Find What** to find which countries have a population between 4 and 5 million.

14. Close the **Find and Replace** box.

15. Leave the table open for the next Driving Lesson.

ⓘ *Wildcards can also be used in queries, see Driving Lesson 58.*

ⓘ *Answers to this exercise can be found at the end of this guide.*

Driving Lesson 36 - Editing Data

▣ Park and Read

Modifying records in a table is a simple task in *Access*. By clicking on the appropriate position and using simple key presses, data may be added, deleted and changed. To edit data, click with the mouse on the appropriate field or move to the field to be edited with the cursor control keys. When the mouse is clicked in a field, a small flashing cursor appears. If **<Tab>** is used to move to the next field, press **<F2>** to view the flashing cursor. This cursor can be moved within the data in a similar way to that in a word processor.

The cursor arrow keys move the cursor left and right by one character. The **<Backspace>** key removes the letter to the left of the cursor. The **<Delete>** or **<Del>** key removes the letter to the right of the cursor.

When a record is being edited, the **Editing Record** indicator, ▨, appears at the left edge of the screen.

⟰ Manoeuvres

1. The **Country** table should still be open. If not, open it.

2. Find the record for **Austria**.

3. Click once with the mouse on the **Population** field. The cursor will appear.

4. Use the left and right cursor keys to move about in the data.

5. Move to the end of the field, i.e. the cursor should be to the right of the 6.

6. Press the **<Backspace>** key to remove the 6.

Australia	Australasia	Canberra	16.4
Austria	Europe	Vienna	7.
Belgium	Europe	Brussels	9.9

7. Type in **7**. Notice that the **Editing Record** indicator appears at the left of the row. The population has now been changed to **7.7**.

8. In a similar way, change the population of the **UK** to **58**.

9. Leave the table on screen for the next Driving Lesson.

Driving Lesson 37 - Undo

Park and Read

It is possible to undo changes made to a record in a database by selecting **Undo**. This will only work for a record that is still currently selected, or if it has been saved and no further changes have been made.

Remember, moving to another record automatically saves changes to the previous one.

The Undo command refers to the last action that was carried out, so it may read **Undo Typing**, **Undo Current Field/Record** *or other commands.*

Manoeuvres

1. Move the cursor into the first field of the **Afghanistan** record and press **<Tab>** to move to the **Region** field. Overtype **Asia** with **Europe**.

2. Press **<Tab>** to move to the **Capital** field. Overtype **Kabul** with **Paris**. Press **<Enter>**.

3. To erase these mistakes, click the **Undo** button, from the **Quick Access Toolbar**. This will undo all amendments made to the current record (Afghanistan is still the current record).

4. **Paris** should now have changed back to **Kabul** and **Europe** to **Asia**.

5. Repeat steps 1 and 2.

6. Click the **Capital** field of **Denmark**. By moving to a different record, the changes for **Afghanistan** have now been saved and it is no longer the current record.

7. Click the **Undo** button, from the **Quick Access Toolbar**. Because no further changes have been made, **Undo** will reverse all amendments made to the last saved record. The changes to the **Afghanistan** record will be corrected.

8. In the **Afghanistan** record, change the **Region** to **Europe**, then in the **Denmark** record, change the **Capital** to **London**, press **<Enter>**.

9. Click the **Undo** button. The changes to the **Denmark** record (the current record) will be reversed.

10. Click **Undo** again. No further reversals are possible.

11. Manually change the **Afghanistan** region back to **Asia**.

12. Close the table and database.

Driving Lesson 38 - Further Editing

▣ Park and Read

Various key presses are available when moving about in text:

←	moves left by 1 character
→	moves right by 1 character
<Ctrl ← >	moves one word to the left
<Ctrl → >	moves one word to the right
<Home>	moves to beginning of field
<End>	moves to end of field

To delete data within the field use the following keys:

<Del>	deletes character at cursor
<Backspace>	deletes character to left of cursor
<Ctrl Backspace>	deletes from cursor to beginning of word

The mouse may also be used to edit by clicking on the required word or letter and dragging to select a block of text to be processed.

⬃ Manoeuvres

1.   Open the **Staff** database and **Courses** table.

2.   Move to the course **Creative Accounting For Beginners** by clicking once on the middle of the field.

3.   The course title is incorrect - it should read **Computer Accounting For Beginners**. Use the left cursor key to move along the line so that it is to the right of the word **Creative**.

4.   Erase **Creative** by using the <**Backspace**> key and type in **Computer**. Press <**Enter**>.

5.   The 4th record reads **Intro to Access**. It should read **Introduction to Access**. Move to the correct field. Move the cursor along the line to the correct position and type **duction**. Press <**Enter**>.

6.   There is an error in the date of the **Virus Writers Workshop**. Move to the **Date** field of record **3**.

7.   Press <**Home**> to move to the beginning of the date. Press <**Delete**> until the date is removed, then enter **15/04/99**. Press <**Enter**>.

8.   Close the table, but leave the database open for the next exercise.

Driving Lesson 39 - Adding/Deleting Records

⊞ Park and Read

Records can easily be inserted into, or deleted from a table. New records are inserted at the bottom of the table, although if a primary key is set or a field is indexed, the record may be in a new position when the table is reopened.

If the cursor is at the end of the table a new record can be added by pressing either <**Enter**> or <**Tab**>.

Manoeuvres

1.   Open the **Staff** table and make sure the **Home** tab is displayed.

2.   Click the **New Record** button, [☞ New] in the **Records** group and create a new record by typing in the following information, pressing <**Tab**> to move into the next field:

        521
        Ms
        Singh
        Ghita
        Sales Manager
        21/6/99
        WF567890G
        30000
        22/7/65

3.   Use your imagination to add another new record for a fictitious person. Remember the validation rules that were set up earlier.

4.   Ghita Singh's record is to be deleted. Position the cursor within her record. Click on the drop down arrow of the **Delete** button, [✕ Delete ▾], on the **Home** tab and select [☞ Delete Record].

        ┌───┐
        │ Microsoft Office Access   [✕] │
        ├───┤
        │   **You are about to delete 1 record(s).**   │
        │   ⚠   If you click Yes, you won't be able to undo this Delete operation. │
        │   Are you sure you want to delete these records? │
        │   │
        │   [Yes   ]   [No   ]   │
        └───┘

5.   Click **Yes** to confirm the deletion.

6.   **Delete** the details for the fictitious person.

7.   Leave the table on screen for the next exercise.

Driving Lesson 40 - Editing Shortcuts

🅿 Park and Read

When editing or entering data, the user may speed up the process by using some "shortcuts" built into *Access*. There are two specific shortcuts supported by the application.

> **<Ctrl '>** This copies the value from the same field of the previous record.

> **<Ctrl ;>** This inserts the current date into the field.

🐾 Manoeuvres

1. **Staff** should still be open from the previous exercise. Add the following new employee.

    802

    Mr

    Miles

    Peter

    Creative Accountant

2. Move to the **Date of Employment** field and use **<Ctrl ;>** to insert today's date.

3. Enter **WL562984T** the **NI Number**.

4. His salary is the same as the previous record, use the **Ditto** function, **<Ctrl '>** (apostrophe) to add the appropriate information.

5. Enter **23/2/75** in the **Date of Birth** field.

6. **Mr Valdron** is, in fact, a typographical error and should be **Mr Waldram**. Move to the appropriate field and correct the mistake.

7. Close the table and database.

Driving Lesson 41 - Revision

This Driving Lesson covers the features introduced in this section. Try not to refer to the preceding Driving Lessons while completing it.

1. Use the **Geography** database and table **Country**.

2. Change **Finland's** population to 6 million.

3. Oops, that was a mistake! **Undo** the changes.

4. Make the **Currency** column about half its original width.

5. Resize any columns so that all information is visible.

6. Add the following record, **Atlantis, Europe, Metropolis, 46, 23, 2, Conch, English**.

UK	Europe	London	57	0.09	602	Pound	English
USA	North America	Washington	248.2	3.6	68	Dollar	English
Atlantis	Europe	Metropolis	46	23	2	Conch	English
*							

7. Change the currency of Atlantis to **Pounds**, and the language to **Spanish**.

8. Use **Find** to locate all the countries within the region **Middle East**. How many are there?

9. Using **Wildcards**, find all capital cities beginning with the letter **B**. How many are there?

10. **Delete** the record for **Atlantis**.

11. Close the table, select **No** at the save prompt.

12. Close the database.

[i] *Answers to this exercise can be found at the end of this guide.*

If you experienced any difficulty completing the Revision, refer back to the Driving Lessons in this section, then re-do the revision.

Driving Lesson 42 - Revision

This Driving Lesson covers the features introduced in this section. Try not to refer to the preceding Driving Lessons while completing it.

1.   Open the database **Houses** and the table **Location**.

2.   **22 Chapel Road** has come on the market. Add a new record – use a keyboard shortcut to copy the details above the new record, remembering to change the address from 21 to 22.

ℹ️   *House Ref* is an AutoNumber field. AutoNumber fields are filled in by Access with the next available sequence number. Start entering new data in the next field, *Type*.

3.   Display the subdatasheets for **21** and **22 Chapel Road**. **22** is slightly cheaper at **£35000**, has the same number of bedrooms, but no garage. It is for sale and unoccupied. Enter this data.

4.   House reference **25** in **Stainburn** should actually read **138 Swaledale Street**. Make the change.

5.   Sorry that was wrong, it should have been **Swaledale Road**, undo the typing and enter the correct address.

6.   **22 Chapel Road** has sold quickly. Delete it from your database.

7.   **44 Daffodil Terrace** has been for sale for some time, so the price is being reduced. Change it to **£27,000**.

8.   The property at **15 Low Row** has been entered as a **First Floor Flat** when in fact it is on the second floor. Make the change.

9.   Close the table, but do not save the changes.

10.   Close the database.

If you experienced any difficulty completing the Revision, refer back to the Driving Lessons in this section, then re-do the revision.

Driving Lesson 43 - Revision

This Driving Lesson covers the features introduced in this section. Try not to refer to the preceding Driving Lessons while completing it.

1.   Open the **Cia** database and the **Customer Details** table.

2.   How many customers live in **County Durham**?

3.   Add a new customer as follows:

      Customer 35, Mr Philip Black of **Black's Beasts, Station Road, Burnley, Lancs, BU3 7GF, Tel 01834 23739, No Fax**

4.   The **Information** field for Mr Black is the same as for the previous record. Use <**Ctrl '**> to copy this data.

5.   Close the table and the database.

6.   Open the **Houses** database and the **Houses** table.

7.   Locate all records that have the word **carpets** somewhere in the **Comment** field. How many are there?

8.   Close the table and the database.

i   *Answers to this exercise can be found at the end of this guide.*

If you experienced any difficulty completing the Revision, refer back to the Driving Lessons in this section, then re-do the revision.

Once you are confident with the features, complete the Record of Achievement Matrix referring to the section at the end of the guide. Only when competent move on to the next Section.

Section 5
Sorting and Filtering

By the end of this Section you should be able to:

Sort Records

Use Filters

To gain an understanding of the above features, work through the **Driving Lessons** in this **Section**.

For each **Driving Lesson**, read the **Park and Read** instructions, without touching the keyboard, then work through the numbered steps of the **Manoeuvres** on the computer. Complete the **Revision Exercise(s)** at the end of the section to test your knowledge.

Driving Lesson 44 - Sorting Records

Park and Read

One of the main features of a powerful database management system is the ability to sort records based on given criteria. This order can be alphabetical, numeric or chronological. Sorts can be carried out in ascending (A-Z, 1-100, etc.) or descending (Z-A, 100-1, etc.) order.

The table is only sorted temporarily. When it is closed and then opened again, the sort is lost. To retain the sort, save the table before closing.

Manoeuvres

1. Open the database **Staff** then the **Staff** table and make sure the **Home** tab is displayed.

2. Click anywhere in the **Surname** field.

3. Click the **Ascending** button, from the **Sort & Filter** group. The table is instantly sorted alphabetically by **Surname**.

*Alternatively, right click in the **Surname** field and click*

4. With the cursor still in the **Surname** field, click the **Descending** button, . Notice how the table is now sorted by surname, in descending order.

5. Sort the table by **Salary** in ascending order.

6. Sort the table by **Salary** in descending order.

7. Sort the table in descending order by the **Date of Employment** to see the newest starters first.

8. Close the table <u>without</u> saving the changes.

9. Close the database.

*The principles of sorting records apply in the same way in **Queries** and **Forms**, see later exercises.*

Driving Lesson 45 - Using Filters

🄿 Park and Read

A filter can be used to find certain information, known as **criteria**. Once the criteria are specified and the filter is applied only the information that fits the criteria will be shown in the table. This data can then be saved, sorted or printed.

👉 Manoeuvres

1. Open the **Geography** database and the table **Country**.

2. Select **Europe** anywhere within the **Region** field and click the **Filter By Selection** button, ⚡ Selection ▾ in the **Sort & Filter** group.

3. Look at the options available and select **Equals "Europe"**. Only countries in Europe are listed. The status bar shows the word **Filtered**.

4. To sort the countries in **Europe** by the size of their population, position the cursor in the **Population** field. Click the **Sort Descending** button, Z↓ A.

5. Click the **Toggle Filter** button, ▽ Toggle Filter, and the **Clear All Sorts** button, 🗛 to return the table to its original state.

6. It is possible to select records *excluding* a certain criteria. Click in a **Currency** field showing **Euro** and click ⚡ Selection ▾.

7. Select **Does Not Equal "Euro"** to list all countries who do not use **Euros**.

8. Click the **Toggle Filter** button to clear the filter then click in the **Population** field for **France**.

9. Click ⚡ Selection ▾ and select **Greater Than or Equal to 55.9**. All countries with a population greater than **France** are listed.

10. Click the **Toggle Filter** button to clear the filter then close the table and database, <u>without</u> saving the changes.

Driving Lesson 46 - Filter by Form

🅿 Park and Read

Another method of using filters is **Filter by Form**. Complex filtering based on more than one field can be built using this technique.

↱ Manoeuvres

1. Open the **Houses** database and the **Houses** table.

2. Click the **Advanced** button, ⌨ Advanced ▾ , from the **Sort & Filter** group on the **Home** tab and select **Filter By Form**.

3. Click in the field under the **Town** heading then click the drop down arrow.

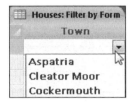

4. Select **Cockermouth**. In the **Type** field, drop down the list and select **Terraced House**.

5. Click the **Advanced** button and select **Apply Filter/Sort** to apply the filter. The table shows **4** terraced houses in Cockermouth.

6. Click **Advanced** then **Filter by Form**.

7. Click in the **Price** field and type **> 30000**.

8. Apply the filter. The table shows **3** terraced houses in Cockermouth costing more than £30,000.

9. Wildcards can be used. Click **Advanced** then **Filter by Form**. Right click in any column and select **Clear Grid** to remove all filters.

10. Type ***bungalow*** in the **Type** field. Apply the filter. This will give all records that include bungalow in their type. There are **5** records.

11. Use **Clear Grid** to remove all filters then type **w*** in the **Town** field. Apply the filter. Properties in any town starting with **W** are listed.

12. Close the table <u>without</u> saving. All filters will be lost.

Driving Lesson 47 - Quick Filters

▣ Park and Read

There are quicker way of filtering which can be applied without using any buttons from the **Ribbon**.

⌒ Manoeuvres

1. Open the **Houses** table in **Datasheet** view. Notice that every column heading has a drop down arrow on the right.

2. Click the drop down arrow for the **Bedrooms** column. The drop down list shows all the different values currently in this column. All are selected by default.

3. Remove the checks for the values **1**, **2** and **3** then click **OK**. The list is filtered to show only properties with **4** or **9** bedrooms.

ⓘ *Further filtering could be applied to this list by selecting filters for other fields.*

4. Display the drop down list again and select **Clear Filter from Bedrooms**. All records are once again listed. Make sure there are no sorts applied, click the **Clear All Sorts** button, ▦ if available.

5. Locate record 13 and right click in the **Type** field (it should be **Bungalow**). A shortcut menu with sorting and filtering options is shown.

6. Select **Contains "Bungalow"**. Only records with the word **bungalow** in the type are listed.

7. Close the table <u>without</u> saving to remove all filters.

Driving Lesson 48 - Revision

This Driving Lesson covers the features introduced in this section. Try not to refer to the preceding Driving Lessons while completing it.

1. Open the **Houses** database and table **Houses**, if it is not already open. Remember to remove the filters between steps.

2. Find all properties in the **Town** of **Whitehaven**.

3. Find all the properties that have **3 bedrooms**.

4. Find all the properties that are in a town beginning with **C**.

5. Find all the properties whose **Type** includes **Flat**. Remember to use the wildcards!

6. Close the table and database <u>without</u> saving the changes.

7. Open the **Geography** database and the table **Country**.

8. How many countries are on the database?

9. How many countries have **English** as their main language?

10. Sort the countries into alphabetical order of their capital city. Which country is first?

11. Remove from view all the records that are in **Europe**? How many records are left?

12. Sort this answer by **Density** – highest first. Which is the most densely populated country outside Europe?

13. Close the table and the database <u>without</u> saving.

[i] *Answers to this exercise can be found at the end of this guide.*

If you experienced any difficulty completing the Revision, refer back to the Driving Lessons in this section, then re-do the revision.

Driving Lesson 49 - Revision

This Driving Lesson covers the features introduced in this section. Try not to refer to the preceding Driving Lessons while completing it.

1. Open the database **Cia** and the table **Prospective Customers**.

2. Sort the table by **Surname** ascending.

3. Use **Filter by Selection** to find how many men are prospective customers.

4. Remove the filter.

5. Close the table and save the sorted order.

6. Open the **Orders** table from the same database.

7. Click the drop down arrow at the top of the **Paid** field and select only those records that have not been paid.

8. Remove the filter to display all records again.

9. Sort the table into **Date Paid** order. This also has the effect of collecting together all of the unpaid invoices.

10. Close the table but do not save it. Close the database.

11. Open the database **Daley** and the table **Vehicles**.

12. Use **Filter by Form** to find out if there are any **Black** cars with an **Engine Capacity** of **3500**.

13. Remove the filter and sort the data by **Engine Capacity** ascending. It does not appear to have sorted in the correct order. Why is this? In **Design View**, try changing the **Field Data Type** for the **Engine Capacity** to **Number** rather than **Text**.

14. Reapply the sort ascending, it should now be correct.

15. Close the table without saving the sorted changes and close the database.

i *Answers to this exercise can be found at the end of this guide.*

If you experienced any difficulty completing the Revision, refer back to the Driving Lessons in this section, then re-do the revision.

Driving Lesson 50 - Revision

This Driving Lesson covers the features introduced in this section. Try not to refer to the preceding Driving Lessons while completing it.

1. Open the **Football Agent** database and the **Current Status** table.

2. Sort the players into order by **Date Joined** showing the longest serving first.

3. Now sort them into salary order, highest paid first.

4. Find the record for **Barry Boots**. Open his subdatasheet and sort the **Date Left** field in descending order. Close the subdatasheet.

i   *This exercise assumes Driving Lesson 31 has been completed. If not, the subdatasheets will not have been created.*

5. Sort the records in **Current Club** order to see if there are any players on the books playing for the same club.

6. Close the table and the database <u>without</u> saving any of the changes - **No to All**.

7. Open the **Staff** database and table.

8. Use a filter to find all staff involved in **sales** (use *sales* in the criteria). How many are there? Remember to remove filters after use.

9. Use **Filter by Form** to find how many men are involved in sales.

10. Use **Filter by Selection** (use the **Between** option) to find all employees who started work in 1985.

11. How many people are paid **£15,000** per annum?

12. Sort by **Date of Birth**. Who is the oldest member of staff?

13. Close the table and database but <u>do not</u> save any changes.

i   *Answers to this exercise can be found at the end of this guide.*

If you experienced any difficulty completing the Revision, refer back to the Driving Lessons in this section, then re-do the revision.

Once you are confident with the features, complete the Record of Achievement Matrix referring to the section at the end of the guide. Only when competent move on to the next Section.

Section 6
Queries

By the end of this Section you should be able to:

Create, Edit and Delete a Query

Use Sort in a Query

Print Query Results

Query Related Tables

Use Value Ranges in Queries

Use a Query to Find Non-Matches

Use AND & OR Queries

To gain an understanding of the above features, work through the **Driving Lessons** in this **Section**.

For each **Driving Lesson**, read the **Park and Read** instructions, without touching the keyboard, then work through the numbered steps of the **Manoeuvres** on the computer. Complete the **Revision Exercise(s)** at the end of the section to test your knowledge.

Driving Lesson 51 - Querying a Table

🄿 Park and Read

A database management system has the ability to process the information the user has entered and produce meaningful results. *Access* uses a system known as **Querying**. A query is used to extract data from a table and analyse that data. Simply create a **Query**, selecting which fields to show in the answer and which records to include. The program then processes the data and performs the query.

Once created, a **Query** can be saved and run whenever required. It will always show the latest data. For example suppose a query is created to list all your customers in a certain town. If new customers are added in that town, the query will immediately reflect this, it does not need to be updated. New fields can be added to queries and existing fields can be removed.

Queries can also be used in place of a table in many instances, e.g. as a basis for **Forms** and **Reports**.

🄸 *There are several types of Query. This guide will only look at simple Select Queries.*

☞ Manoeuvres

1. Open the database **Mailing**, select the **Create** tab and click **Query Design** in the **Other** group. The **Show Table** dialog box is displayed and shows a list of available tables.

    Query Design

    ```
    Show Table                           ? ✖

     Tables  Queries  Both

      Mailing
      New Mail
    
    
    
    
    
    
    
    
    
                              Add      Close
    ```

2. Select **Mailing** as the required table, click **Add** and then **Close**.

☞

Driving Lesson 51 - Continued

3. The **Select Query** window is now visible. Notice the **Field List** in the top half of the window which shows the available fields, and the **Query Grid** in the bottom half which shows which fields will be included in the output.

4. There are several ways to move fields from the **Field List** to the **Query Grid**. In the **Field List**, click on **Name** and drag it down to the **Query Grid**. Release it anywhere in the first column.

5. The **Show** box should be checked (have a tick in it) to indicate that this field is required in the output list.

It is possible to use a field in a Query for selection purposes without showing it in the output.

6. To run the query, display the **Design** tab and click the **Run** button. A results table appears. In this case it only consists of the **Name** field because that was the only field placed on to the **Query Grid**.

7. The query results table act exactly like any other table. Use the navigation buttons to navigate between the records as before.

8. To switch back to the query design, make sure the **Home** tab is displayed and click the **Design View** button.

9. In the second column of the **Query Grid**, display the drop down list in the first field and select **Department** from the list of available fields.

10. Click the **Run** button. Both **Name** and **Department** will now be listed. Switch back to the query design, using the **Design View** button and leave the query open for the next Driving Lesson.

Driving Lesson 52 - Selecting in Queries

▣ Park and Read

One of the main uses of a query is to select certain records from a table based on entered criteria.

☞ Manoeuvres

1. In the query from the last exercise, double click on **Organisation** in the **Field List**. The field is added to the next empty column in the **Query Grid**.

2. To select records for only certain organisations, click in the **Criteria** field for this column, type **school** and press the **<Enter>** key.

Field:	Name	Department	Organisation
Table:	Mailing	Mailing	Mailing
Sort:			
Show:	☑	☑	☑
Criteria:			"school"
or:			

3. Notice the quotes around the **school** criteria. *Access* often changes the criteria to its own language. Run the query. The query lists the three requested fields for all records with an **Organisation** value of **School**.

ℹ *Querying is <u>not</u> case sensitive. Searching for Fred will also find FRED and fred.*

4. Use the **Design View** button to switch back to query design.

5. Click in the **Organisation** column of the **Query Grid** and from the **Design** tab click ⚞ Delete Columns. The column is removed.

6. Remove the **Department** column from the **Query Grid** in the same way.

7. Use any method to place the fields **Town** and **Post code** into the second and third columns of the **Query Grid**.

8. In the **Criteria** of the **Town** field, type **London**. Run the query. It lists name and postcodes of people living in London. There are **2** records.

9. Right click on the tab header for this query and select **Close**.

10. A message will be displayed asking if you want to save the changes to this query. Click **No**. The query will be closed without saving and therefore cannot be used again.

11. Close the database.

Driving Lesson 53 - Sorting Query Results

◨ Park and Read

Query results may be easier to understand if they are placed in a certain order or sorted. It is also a useful tool when query results are used in reports.

♘ Manoeuvres

1. Open the database **Houses**, select the **Create** tab and click **Query Design**. The **Show Table** dialog box is displayed and shows a list of available tables.

2. Add the **Houses** table to the query and close the dialog box.

3. In the **Field List** for **Houses**, click on **Town**. Move down the list, hold down <Shift>, and click on **Price**. Five fields should now be selected. Click in the selection and drag down to the first column of the query grid, then release the mouse button. All of the fields should be visible in the query grid with their **Show** boxes checked.

4. Delete the column for **Occupied**. then in the **Criteria** for **Town**, enter **Cockermouth**. Run the query. There are **5** results.

5. To sort these in order of price, first use the **Design View** button to switch back to query design.

6. In the **Sort** area for **Price**, drop down the list.

Field:	Town	Address	Type	Price	
Table:	Houses	Houses	Houses	Houses	
Sort:					▼
Show:	☑	☑	☑	Ascending	
Criteria:	"Cockermouth"			Descending	
or:				(not sorted)	

7. Select **Ascending** and run the query again. Records for properties in Cockermouth are listed in ascending order of price.

8. Switch back to **Design View** again, add **Bedrooms** to the **Query Grid** and delete the contents of the **Criteria** field for **Town**.

9. In the **Criteria** for **Bedrooms** enter **2** and sort the **Price** field in **Descending** order.

Field:	Town	Address	Type	Price	Bedrooms
Table:	Houses	Houses	Houses	Houses	Houses
Sort:				▼	
Show:	☑	☑	☑	Ascending	☑
Criteria:				Descending	2
or:				(not sorted)	

10. Run the query - the table shows 9 houses with exactly two bedrooms, sorted by price, most expensive first. Leave the query open.

Driving Lesson 54 - Saving Query Results

◻ Park and Read

Queries can be saved so that when data changes, the query can be run again to reflect the changes, without the necessity of redesigning it.

↝ Manoeuvres

1. Right click on the tab header for the query created in the previous Driving Lesson and select **Save**. The **Save As** dialog box is displayed.

2. Replace the text **Query1** with **2 Bedrooms** and click **OK**. The query is saved and the title is shown in the tab header for this query. The **Navigation** pane now shows the saved query **2 Bedrooms** (if **All Access Objects** is selected).

3. Return to **Design View** and sort the **Town** field as **Ascending** leaving all other criteria as they are. Run the query.

4. Notice that the first sort is alphabetically by town. The second sort is on price in descending order, so within each town group, the records are sorted with the highest price first.

5. Return to **Design View** and change the **Town** field sort to **Descending**. Run the query to see the towns in reverse alphabetical order.

6. Use the **Close** button, ☒, to close the query. At the dialog box select **No**. The query is closed without saving and the recent changes are lost.

7. Double click on the **2 Bedrooms** query from the **Navigation** pane to open it. It is the version that was saved at step 2.

8. Leave the query open for the next Driving Lesson.

Driving Lesson 55 - Printing Query Results

⊞ Park and Read

When a hard copy of query results is required, it is a simple matter to print out the results.

↷ Manoeuvres

1. The **2 Bedrooms** query is open from the previous Driving Lesson. To see a preview of how the query will appear when printed, click the **Office Button** and move the cursor over **Print** to display printing options.

ⓘ *Select* ***Quick Print****, from the* ***Office Button*** *menu to print directly without displaying the* ***Print*** *dialog box.*

2. Select **Print Preview** from the options. A **Print Preview** tab is displayed in the **Ribbon** and the query results are displayed as they will print.

3. Note that the print has a header showing the title of the query and the date, and a footer showing the page number. Zoom in to the page by clicking on it with the magnifier.

4. Click the **Landscape** button on the **Print Preview** tab to change the orientation of the print on the page.

5. Click the **Print** button, or use the key press **<Ctrl P>**, to open the **Print** dialog box. The dialog box has options to print selected parts of the query result, in exactly the same way as for a table. There is also an option to print more than one copy.

6. Click **OK** to print a single copy of the whole list.

7. Use the button on the **Ribbon** to **Close Print Preview**.

8. Close the **2 Bedrooms** query and close the database.

Driving Lesson 56 - Querying Related Tables

Park and Read

The technique for querying related tables is exactly the same as for one, except that at the **Show Table** stage, more than one table may be added.

Fields can then be chosen from both tables to give a result that would not be possible from an individual table.

Manoeuvres

1. Open the database **Daley**.

2. Display the **Create** tab and select **Query Design**.

3. The **Show Table** dialog box lists all available tables. Double click on **Vehicles** and then on **Repairs** to add them to the query. Close the **Show Table** dialog box.

4. The relationships between the tables were set in Driving Lesson 28 and are shown here.

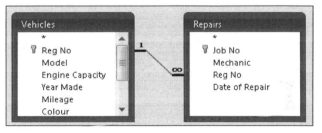

If Driving Lesson 28 has not been completed and there is no existing relationship, it can be defined on this screen but will only apply to this query.

5. From the **Vehicles** field list add the following fields: **Reg No**, **Model** and **Manufacturer**.

6. From the **Repairs** field list add the following fields: **Mechanic** and **Date of Repair**.

Field:	Reg No	Model	Manufacturer	Mechanic	Date of Repair	
Table:	Vehicles	Vehicles	Vehicles	Repairs	Repairs	
Sort:						
Show:	☑	☑	☑	☑	☑	
Criteria:						
or:						

7. Note that the **Table** name for each field is displayed in the query, indicating the source of each of the fields.

Driving Lesson 56 - Continued

8. In the **Mechanic** criteria enter **David**. This will display only David's jobs. Run the query. There are **2** records.

9. There really is no need to display David's name in the result as all the information applies to him. Switch back to **Design View** and click in the **Show** box for **Mechanic**. The tick ☑ is removed.

10. Run the query again. The results are the same, except that David's name is not shown.

ⓘ *The field has not been removed from the query. It can still be used for selection or sorting purposes.*

11. To 'unhide' the field, return to **Design View** and replace the tick in the **Show** box. Run the query again, the name will be shown.

12. Return to **Design View**, remove the tick from the **Show** box in the **Mechanic** field and save the query as **David**.

13. Run the query and **Print Preview** the query results. David's name will appear as the title.

14. Print a copy.

ⓘ *When a query includes data from 2 tables, records will only be included in the results where there is corresponding data from both tables. In the example above, if there is a vehicle that has no repair jobs, it will not appear in the results.*

15. Return to **Design View**, move the cursor above the **Date of Repair** field until the cursor changes to a black downward arrow, and click once to select the whole column.

16. Press the <**Delete**> key to remove the field. It can no longer be used for selection or sorting. Run the query to see the effect.

17. Close the query without saving but leave the database open.

Driving Lesson 57 - Editing Queries

Park and Read

There may be occasions when several similar queries are required. It is usual in these circumstances to edit the original query, rather than set up and save new ones. For example, if in an address query the only criterion that changes is the beginning of the postcode, then it is acceptable to run the query for one postcode, print or preview the result, before editing the query for another postcode. The amended queries can be saved with a different name if required.

Fields appear in the results in the order they appear in the Query Grid and they can be moved to a more suitable position in the grid if required.

Manoeuvres

1. The **Daley** database is open, open the **David** query.

2. Switch to **Design View**. Exactly the same information is required for Richard. Change the criteria for the **Mechanic** to **Richard**.

3. Run the query. This time Richard's details are shown. If a printout is required however, the printout will still show David as the title.

4. Click the **Office** button and select **Save As**.

5. Change the name from **Copy of David** to **Richard** and click **OK**. A second query is saved with a name of **Richard**.

6. Switch to **Design View**. It makes more sense to have the Manufacturer's name before the Model name. Move the cursor above the **Manufacturer** field until the cursor changes to a black downward arrow, and click once to select the column.

7. Point the cursor in the narrow black area above the field name until it changes to a white arrow and drag the field to the position between **Model** and **Reg No**. A thick black line will help you.

Field:	Reg No	Manufacturer	Model	Mechanic
Table:	Vehicles	Vehicles	Vehicles	Repairs
Sort:				
Show:	☑	☑	☑	☐
Criteria:				"Richard"
or:				

8. Once the mouse button is released the field is dropped in its new position.

9. Run the query then close it without saving but leave the database open.

Driving Lesson 58 - Ranges of Values and Wildcards

▣ Park and Read

When you want to perform a query that does not contain precise values, or contains an unknown element, you can use **ranges of values** and **wildcards**. The following search rules apply to queries run on single or related tables.

A range of values can be specified in a query using the following operators:

>	Greater than	**<**	Less than
>=	Greater than / equal to	**<=**	Less than / equal to

These operators allow the user to process data depending on its order. As with exact matches, the required range is typed into the appropriate field of the query grid. For example, to discover which items, if any, are in short supply in a table of stock records, the user could type **<100** in the **Stock Level** field of the query grid to display all the items with less than 100 in stock.

Wildcards can be used in queries to search for patterns in data, e.g. all employees whose last names begin with **Mac** or end with **son**. The following wildcard characters are used:

　* to replace one or more characters (**%** if using ANSI-92 SQL)

　? to replace a single character (**_** if using ANSI-92 SQL)

For example, wildcards could be used to select 'Sales' people from their job titles, which may be sales assistant, sales supervisor, etc.

☞ Manoeuvres

1.　Use the database **Daley** and create a query using the **Vehicles** table.

2.　Place the **Reg No**, **Model** and **Price** fields on to the query grid.

3.　To find all the cars costing less than £3000, type **<3000** in the criteria box of the **Price** field. Make sure that the **Show** boxes are checked.

Field:	Reg No	Model	Price
Table:	Vehicles	Vehicles	Vehicles
Sort:			
Show:	☑	☑	☑
Criteria:			<3000
or:			

4.　**Run** the query. The answer table should contain the vehicles costing less than £3000 and display their **Reg No**, **Model** and **Price**. Click on **Design View** to return to the **Query Grid**.

☞

Driving Lesson 58 - Continued

5. Multiple selection criteria can be entered in the same query. Add the **Previous owners** field to the query grid. To look for all cars with four or more owners, <u>and</u> which also cost less than £3000. Type **>=4** in the criteria box for **Previous owners**.

6. Run the query. This is a multiple query, it has more than one selection criteria. Because <u>both</u> criteria must be met for a record to be selected, this is an example of an AND query.

7. Save the query as **Owners** and click **OK**. Close the query and the database.

8. Open the **Houses** database and create a new query in **Design View** based on the **Houses** table.

9. Place the **Town**, **Address**, **Type**, **Price** and **Comment** fields into the query grid.

10. We need to search for properties where **detached** or **semi-detached** is a feature in the **Type** field. The properties may be houses, bungalows, etc. The text may appear in a variety of forms, e.g. **semi-detached house**, **detached bungalow**, and may be in the middle of other text.

11. In the criteria row for the **Type** field, type ***detached***. This is enough information to find all required occurrences because the wildcard characters, (*), denote that any amount of text may occur before or after the selected characters (If this doesn't work, use **%detached%**).

12. Press <**Enter**> and note that *Access* changes the criteria to **Like "*detached*"**, which is the code it uses to perform a wildcard search.

13. Run the query. Records are found with a variety of relevant **Type** fields.

Town	Address	Type	Price	Comment
Cockermouth	8 Blackpool Court	Detached House	£38,000	Quiet Road
Aspatria	15 Waldram Way	Semi-Detached House	£39,000	Quiet Road
Great Broughton	The Castle	Detached House	£47,000	Conservatory
Workington	1 Whitburn Street	Semi-Detached House	£17,000	Includes Carpets
Whitehaven	9 Deepdene	Detached House	£49,950	Listed Building
Whitehaven	25 Lilac Close	Detached House	£58,950	Panoramic Views
High Seaton	6 Stonehills	Detached Bungalow	£55,000	Inc.Carpets & Curtains
Workington	265 Harrison Road	Semi-Detached House	£16,500	Poor Decorative Order
Stainburn	138 Swaledale	Detached House	£47,500	Includes Carpets
Workington	21 Chapel Road	Semi-Detached House	£36,950	Well Maintained

Record: 1 of 10   No Filter   Search

14. Switch back to **Design View**. Delete the criteria in the **Type** field and type ***r?ad** in the criteria for the **Address** field.

15. Run the query. All records where the address ends in **road** (or read or riad, etc.) will be listed. (If this doesn't work, use **%r_ad**).

16. Close the query without saving and close the **Houses** database.

Driving Lesson 59 - Non-Matches

▣ Park and Read

In order to produce results which exclude the matches made using other searches, the user may precede any criteria with the operator **<>** or **NOT**, as in not London, or not *sales*, or <> Scotland.

⟲ Manoeuvres

1. Open the database **Houses** and create a new query using both the **Location** and **House details** tables.

2. Place the **Town** and **Type** from the **Location** table and **Price** from the **House details** table on to the query grid. Ensure that they have their **Show** boxes checked.

3. In the **Criteria** box for the **Town** field, type **Not Cockermouth** to find all the properties except those in Cockermouth.

4. **Run** the query. The answer table contains 25 records.

5. Switch to the **Query Design**. In the **Town Criteria** box change the entry to **<> Workington**

6. Add the **Address** field to the query grid and sort the query by **Town** (ascending) and then **Price** (ascending). **Run** the query. There are now 24 results.

7. Save the query as **Not Workington**.

8. Preview the results before printing a copy.

9. Close the query and the database.

ℹ️ *Access does not select blank fields when searching for non-matches. For example a record with no data in the **Town** field, would <u>not</u> be included in a **Not Workington** query.*

Driving Lesson 60 - And Queries

🄿 Park and Read

Previous Driving Lessons have demonstrated **AND** queries with selections in different fields. When it is necessary that two conditions must be met in a single field, e.g. a value must be higher than one value and lower than another, then the word **and** is used. Simply enter the two queries in the field, separated by the word **and**. As an alternative, the function **Between** can be used.

Manoeuvres

1. Open the database **Staff** and create a new query using the **Staff** table.

2. Place the fields **Surname** and **Date of Birth** on to the grid.

3. To list all the employees born in the 1960s, type the following information into the **Date of Birth Criteria** box and press <**Enter**>.

    >=01/01/60 and <=31/12/69

4. Widen the **Date of Birth** field by clicking and dragging the right border to the right, until all the data is visible.

Field:	Surname	Date of Birth	
Table:	Staff List	Staff List	
Sort:			
Show:	☑	☑	
Criteria:		> =#01/01/1960# And < =#31/12/1969#	
or:			

5. **Run** the query. The list contains the names of all the people born in the 1960s (about 8 records, depending on values used on additional records).

6. Switch back to the query design. Remove the **Date of Birth** field from the grid by highlighting the column and selecting **Delete Columns**.

7. Place the **Salary** field on to the query grid.

8. To find everyone who earns between £15,000 and £20,000 type **between 15000 and 20000** in the **Criteria** box of the **Salary** column.

Field:	Surname	Salary	
Table:	Staff List	Staff List	
Sort:			
Show:	☑	☑	
Criteria:		Between 15000 And 20000	
or:			

9. **Run** the query. The list contains all of the people who earn between £15,000 and £20,000 (6 records).

10. Close the query <u>without</u> saving and close the database.

Driving Lesson 61 - Or Queries

🅿 Park and Read

If a value within a particular field needs to match one of two or more conditions, then the conditions may be entered into the appropriate field on the query grid separated by **Or**. They may also be on displayed on separate lines in the query grid. **AND** and **OR** queries are examples of **logical operators**.

🖙 Manoeuvres

1. Using the **Houses** database, create a new query grid based on the **Houses** table, including the fields **Town**, **Address** and **Bedrooms**.

2. To search for all properties in Maryport **Or** Aspatria, enter **Maryport or Aspatria** in the **Criteria** box for **Town**.

Field:	Town	Address	Bedrooms
Table:	Houses	Houses	Houses
Sort:			
Show:	✓	✓	✓
Criteria:	"Maryport" Or "Aspatria"		
or:			

3. **Run** the query. The answer table contains all properties in Maryport or Aspatria. There are 5. Switch back to the query design.

4. Clear the **Town** criteria and in the **Criteria** box of the **Bedrooms** field enter **3**. In the line below, the **or** line, enter **4**. This will search for three <u>or</u> four bedroom houses.

Field:	Town	Address	Bedrooms
Table:	Houses	Houses	Houses
Sort:			
Show:	✓	✓	✓
Criteria:			3
or:			4

5. **Run** the query. The answer table contains eighteen properties, all of which have either three or four bedrooms.

6. Switch back to the query design and change the criteria as shown.

Field:	Town	Address	Bedrooms
Table:	Houses	Houses	Houses
Sort:			
Show:	✓	✓	✓
Criteria:	"Maryport"		
or:			4

7. Run the query. The results contain all properties which are either in Maryport <u>or</u> have 4 bedrooms.

8. Save the query as **Complex** and close it, but leave the database open.

Driving Lesson 62 - Deleting a Query

▣ Park and Read

When several queries have been run and saved, the **Database Window** may become cluttered. In this instance, it is a good idea to delete those no longer required.

Care should be taken, however, that the queries being deleted are not used elsewhere, i.e. a form or report may be based on a particular query, deleting it will render the form/report unusable.

⌕ Manoeuvres

1. The **Houses** database is open from the previous driving lesson. If the **Navigation** pane is showing **All Access Objects**, the three queries created in this section will be listed.

Queries	≫
▦ 2 Bedrooms	
▦ Complex	
▦ Not Workington	

2. From the list of **3** saved queries, click on **Not Workington**.

3. Press the **<Delete>** key or click the **Delete** button in the **Records** group of the **Home** tab. A dialog box is displayed.

    Microsoft Office Access

    ⚠ Do you want to delete the query 'Not Workington'? Deleting this object will remove it from all groups.

    For more information on how to prevent this message from displaying every time you delete an object, click Help.

    [Yes]   [No]   [Help]

4. Select **Yes** to confirm the deletion.

5. Leave the database open for the next Driving Lesson.

Driving Lesson 63 - Revision

This Driving Lesson covers the features introduced in this section. Try not to refer to the preceding Driving Lessons while completing it.

1.   The database **Houses** is open from the previous Driving Lesson. Create a new query using the **Houses** table.

2.   In the **Field List**, select all the fields and place them on the query grid.

3.   Search for all properties in the table located in **Cockermouth**.

4.   **Run** the query and view the answer table.

5.   Switch back to the query design. Clear the grid. Now try the following questions. The fields to use are shown in brackets after each question.

6.   How many properties include a garage in the sale? Place **Yes** in the **Garage** column. (Show **Town**, **Address** and **Garage**).

7.   How many properties are for sale? Put **For Sale** in the **Status** field. (Show **Town**, **Address**, **Price** and **Status**).

8.   How many three-bedroom properties are there? (Show **Town**, **Address**, **Bedrooms** and **Price**).

9.   How many properties are there in **Whitehaven**? (Show **Town**, **Address** and **Price**).

10. How many properties cost less than £22,000? (Show **Town**, **Address**, **Price**).

11. How many properties cost between £40,000 and £50,000? (Show **Town**, **Address**, **Price**).

12. Use the criteria ***list*** in the **Comment** field. What comment does it find, and what is the Address? (Show **Town**, **Address**, **Comment**).

13. Use **<> None** in the **Offers** column, to discover how many houses have offers placed on them. (Show **Town**, **Address**, **Offers**).

14. Close the query <u>without</u> saving.

15. Close the database.

i   *Answers to this exercise can be found at the end of this guide.*

If you experienced any difficulty completing the Revision, refer back to the Driving Lessons in this section, then re-do the revision.

Driving Lesson 64 - Revision

This Driving Lesson covers the features introduced in this section. Try not to refer to the preceding Driving Lessons while completing it.

1. Open the **Football Agent** database and create a query that will show the **Surname**, **First name**, **Current Club** and **Annual salary** of any player earning more than £100,000 per year. Do not show the actual salary.

2. Move the **First name** field so that it will be displayed before the **Surname**.

3. Print a copy of the result but do not save the query.

4. Close the database.

5. Open the database **Daley** and create a new query.

6. All tables are to be included in the query.

7. Create a query to show the manufacturer and model of all cars repaired on 2nd January 2002 and who the mechanic was for each job.

8. Save the query as **2 Jan**.

9. Do not show the date in the answer, as it will now be the title of the query result. Print a copy.

10. Delete this query and close the database.

11. Open the **Staff** database and create a new query based on the **Staff** and **Courses** tables.

12. Find out how many staff have been on a course after the 1st April 1995. Show **Title**, **First name**, **Surname**, **Course** and **Date**.

13. Using the same fields, find out how many staff have been on an introductory course of some kind – use *intro* as the criteria.

14. Find out the only member of staff with a salary of more than £20,000 has been on an Intermediate course.

15. Close the query <u>without</u> saving and close the database.

[i] *Answers to this exercise can be found at the end of this guide.*

If you experienced any difficulty completing the Revision, refer back to the Driving Lessons in this section, then re-do the revision.

Once you are confident with the features, complete the Record of Achievement Matrix referring to the section at the end of the guide. Only when competent move on to the next Section.

Section 7
Forms

By the end of this Section you should be able to:

Create Quick Forms

Design and Create a New Form

Format a Form

Edit and Delete a Form

Edit and Browse Data within a Form

Print from a Form

To gain an understanding of the above features, work through the **Driving Lessons** in this **Section**.

For each **Driving Lesson**, read the **Park and Read** instructions, without touching the keyboard, then work through the numbered steps of the **Manoeuvres** on the computer. Complete the **Revision Exercise(s)** at the end of the section to test your knowledge.

Driving Lesson 65 - Forms

▣ Park and Read

Datasheet View is the default setting for looking at a table. It shows many records at a time in a fixed format, but for large records in particular it will not show all of the fields without scrolling. **Forms** usually show the information one record at a time, but can display all of the fields on the screen at once.

Extra information and functionality can be added to forms, such as graphics, text and validation. Records can be displayed, amended, added or deleted and forms can be formatted to change the appearance, order and number of fields displayed, making them very useful for data entry tasks or for enquiry screens.

⌒ Manoeuvres

1. Open the database **Houses**. Open the **Houses** table in **Datasheet View** and examine the structure. Scrolling will be required to see all the fields in a record, unless you have a very large screen. Close the **Houses** table.

2. Locate the **House Data** form in the **Forms** section of the **Navigation** pane. Double click on the **House Data** form to open it.

3. This form shows all of the fields from the **Houses** table, but because it shows only one record at a time, all fields are visible on the same screen.

4. Look at the form. This was produced as a quick form and then some extra formatting was added. Compared to using the original **Datasheet** view, this is a better way to add records or examine all the data for a record.

5. Use the navigation buttons at the bottom of the form to view other records.

6. Close the **House Data** form but leave the database open.

Driving Lesson 66 - Quick Forms

▣ Park and Read

Access includes a function to create simple forms quickly, based on any selected table or query. Once created, the design of the forms produced can be altered in **Design** or **Layout** view.

☞ Manoeuvres

1.   The **Houses** database should be open. In the **Navigation** panel, click the table **House details** to select it.

2.   Select the **Create** tab on the **Ribbon**, then click the **Form** button. A quick form is created based on the selected table, **House Details**.

House details
House details
House Ref:	1
Occupied:	Yes
Price:	£38,000
Bedrooms:	9
Garage:	Yes
Offer Price:	
Status:	For Sale

Record: ◄ ◄ 1 of 30 ► ►► ◄ No Filter Search

ⓘ *A Quick form is based on whichever table or query is selected at the time.*

3.   Notice that when the form was created there was no input from the user regarding the appearance of the form. All fields from the table are displayed in the form.

4.   Now that the form is created however, it can be amended. By default the new form is shown in **Layout** view. Fields can be added, moved and deleted in this view. Click in the **Occupied** field to select it.

ⓘ *If all fields are already selected, click away from them to remove the selection.*

☞

Driving Lesson 66 - Continued

5.   Press the <**Delete**> key. The field is removed.

6.   Click the **Form** view button , on the **Format** tab to display the form
       in its operating mode.

7.   Click the **Office** button in the top left corner of the *Access* screen
       and click **Save As**. Save the form as **House details** then close it.

8.   Quick forms can be created in different layouts. Click on the **Houses** table
       to select it.

9.   Select the **Create** tab on the **Ribbon**, then click the **Split Form**
       button. A different kind of quick form is created based on the
       selected table, **Houses**.

Houses			
Town:	Cockermouth	Garden:	Large
Address:	8 Blackpool Court	Heating:	Gas
Type:	Detached House	Glazed:	Yes
Occupied:	Yes	Comment:	Quiet Road
Price:	£38,000	Offers:	Mr James 37,250
Bedrooms:	9	Status:	For Sale
Garage:	Yes		

Town	Address	Type	Occupied	Price
Cockermouth	8 Blackpool Court	Detached House	Yes	£38,000
Aspatria	15 Waldram Way	Semi-Detached House	Yes	£39,000
Great Broughton	The Castle	Detached House	Yes	£47,000
Workington	1 Peel Street	Ground Floor Flat	No	£15,000
Frizington	20 High Street	Terraced Cottage	Yes	£10,000
Cockermouth	1 Poplar Place	Terraced House	Yes	£36,700

       Record: 1 of 30   No Filter   Search

10.   This has a **Datasheet** view of all records in the lower part of the form, and
       a form view of the selected record in the upper part. Scroll down the
       Datasheet view until the record for **9 Deepdene** is seen in the list. Click
       on the record to display its details in full in the upper part of the form.

11.   Close the form <u>without</u> saving but leave the database open.

Driving Lesson 67 - Form Wizard

▣ Park and Read

Another method of creating a form is to use the wizard. This gives step by step help in the creation of the form and allows more variety in the layout and the format.

Manoeuvres

1. The **Houses** database should still be open.

2. Select the **Create** tab and click on **More Forms**.

3. Click **Form Wizard** from the list.

4. The first dialog box of the **Form Wizard** is displayed. Make sure the **Houses** table is selected as the source of data (**Table/Queries**). Select from the drop down list if necessary.

5. Click >> to place all of the available fields on the form. A choice of individual fields could be made using > instead if required. By selecting fields individually in a different order they can be made to appear on the form in that order.

6. Click on **Next**.

Driving Lesson 67 - Continued

7. Click each layout to view the sample. Select **Columnar** and click **Next**.

8. View the various options for the style. Select **Foundry** and click **Next**.

9. Enter **Houses Wizard** as the form title.

10. Click **Finish** to create and save the form.

11. Scroll through the records using the navigation buttons, then click the drop down arrow on the **Views** button and switch to **Design** view to see the design of the form.

12. Close the form and the database.

Driving Lesson 68 - Designing a Form

▶ Park and Read

Forms can be created manually from fields in tables or queries. **Layout** view allows the form to be assembled and amended whilst the actual data is being displayed, which is useful when setting field sizes for example. In **Design** view only the field definitions are shown, but the form layout is shown in more detail and a greater range of changes are possible.

▶ Manoeuvres

1. Open the database **Mailing** and the table **Mailing**. Select the **Create** tab and click the **Blank Form** button. A blank form opens in **Layout** view with a list of available fields from the **Mailing** table on the right.

2. In the field list, double click on the **Name** field. It is placed on the form.

3. Double click on the **Department** field, then on the **Town** field. These are placed on the form in order under the first field. A simple form can be built in this way.

4. Close the form <u>without</u> saving.

5. Select the **Create** tab and click the **Form Design** button. A blank form opens in **Design** view with a list of available fields on the right.

ℹ️ *If the **Field List** is not seen it can be displayed by clicking the **Add Existing Fields** button.*

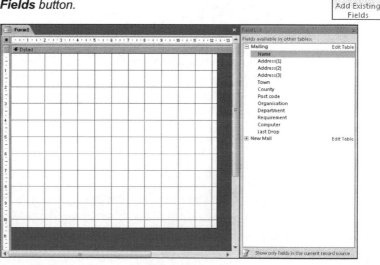

Driving Lesson 68 - Continued

6. Move the mouse pointer over the bottom edge of the form grid. The mouse pointer will change to a double-headed arrow, ⬍. Over the bottom right corner of the form, it changes to a four headed arrow, ✛. Clicking and dragging the edges of the form, changes its shape.

7. Click and drag the form until it is **13cm** wide and **7cm** high (use the rulers as a guide).

8. Click the top field in the **Field List, Name**. Click and drag this field on to the form, releasing the mouse button in the top of the form. Note that the mouse pointer changes when dragged.

9. Two boxes appear on the form. The first is the text label, **Name** and the second is the field that will show the data from the record. Click on the edge of the data field, and drag it to the left half of the form.

10. Click and drag **Department** from the **Field List** on to the form, and position it to the right of the **Name** field on the form.

11. Click the second field in the list, **Address(1)**. Hold the <**Shift**> key and click **Post code**. This selects all fields from **Address(1)** to **Post code**.

12. Click and drag the block of fields on to the form. Release the mouse button in the centre of the form, just below the **Name** field. The form should look similar to that below.

Name:		Name		Department:	Department	
		Address(1):		Address(1)		
		Address(2):		Address(2)		
		Address(3):		Address(3)		
		Town:		Town		
		County:		County		
		Post code:		Post code		

13. Use the **View** button to switch to **Layout** view.

14. Click and drag the right edge of the **Address(1)** field (not the label) to enlarge the field and see all the data. Repeat for **Address(2)**.

15. Click on the **Department** label and press <**Delete**>.

16. Move the **Name** label, the **Name** field and the **Department** field closer together on the line.

17. Right click on the form object tab and save it as **Addresses**. Leave the form on screen for the next exercise.

Driving Lesson 69 - Editing Form Design

Park and Read

Once forms have been created they can be easily edited, e.g. to change the arrangement of objects within the form layout.

Manoeuvres

1.   The **Addresses** form is still visible in **Design View**. Switch to **Form View** to view the data. Switch back to **Design View**.

2.   Click the **Select All** button, , from the **Controls** group or press **<Ctrl A>** to select all fields on the form.

3.   Position the mouse over one of the fields. Click and drag any field slightly to move all of them.

4.   Select the **Arrange** tab and click the **Form Header/Footer** button , in the **Show/Hide** group. Two new areas appear in the form grid.

5.   Select the **Design** tab and from the **Controls** group, click the **Label** tool,

     Aa
     Label . Click and drag with the **Label** pointer, , to create a box in the centre of the **Form Header**, about **5cm** by **1cm** – use the ruler as a guide.

6.   The box has an insertion point in it. Type in **CIA Addresses**. Click outside the box to check the appearance of the text. Click the box again to display the handles.

7.   There are formatting commands in the **Font** group of the **Design** tab that can be used to change text appearance. The formatting will apply to all text in any selected boxes.

8.   Experiment by changing the font, size, appearance and alignment of the text in the label box. End with the text large, bold and centred. Try formatting some of the other labels and fields.

9.   View the **Form Footer**. Click and drag the bottom edge of the footer upwards to reduce its size to about **1cm**. Use the **Label** tool to add a box containing the word **Confidential**.

10. Click the **Form Header** label box and amend the text to **CIA Mailing List**. Resize the **Form Header** area so that the label box just fits in.

11. Save the form and leave on screen for the next Driving Lesson.

Driving Lesson 70 - Sorting and Editing Records

🅿 Park and Read

Once a form has been created, records can be entered/browsed in the same way as in **Datasheet View**. Once information has been entered, it is automatically saved into the database. Any messages regarding saving the form are referring to the format of the form and not the data entered.

To view records, use the **Record Navigation** buttons or press <F5> to go to a specific record.

Use Ⓐ↓ and Ⓩ↓ to sort the information.

👆 Manoeuvres

1. Switch to **Form View** for the **Addresses** form in the **Mailing** database.

> **Addresses**
>
> ### CIA Mailing List
>
> Name: Brian George   Technology
>
> Address(1): William Hill School
> Address(2): Steetchley Avenue
> Address(3):
> Town: Worcester
> County:
> Post code: WR5 2DE
>
> CONFIDENTIAL
>
> Record: 14 ◄ 1 of 19 ► ►I ► No Filter Search

Record Navigation buttons

2. Click the **New Record** button, , to start a new record. Enter your **Name**, **Address**, **Organisation** and **Department** into the blank fields, using <Tab> or <Enter> to move between the fields. Complete the last field, or press **New Record** again, to add the new record, record 20.

3. **Navigation** buttons can be used to move through the records. Click the **Previous** record button, ◄, 3 times to move to record 17, then the **Next** record button, ►, to move to record 18.

👉

Driving Lesson 70 - Continued

4. Move to the last record using . On the **Home** tab, click the drop down arrow on the **Delete** button and select Delete Record.

> **Microsoft Office Access**
>
> ⚠ **You are about to delete 1 record(s).**
>
> If you click Yes, you won't be able to undo this Delete operation. Are you sure you want to delete these records?
>
> [Yes]   [No]

5. Click **Yes** at the warning message.

6. Use to move to the first record. Click in **Address (1)** field and press the **Ascending** button, . The first record is now that of **Andrews High School**.

7. Leaving the cursor in the same field, press the **Descending** button, . The first record is now **Wills School**.

8. Sort the records by **Town** – ascending. The first town will be **Brighton**.

9. Press the **Clear All Sorts** button, . All sorts are removed and the records will be in their original order.

10. To display a specifically numbered record, click in the record number area of the **Navigation** buttons and delete the current record number.

> Record: ◄ ◄ [   ] ► ►◄ ►＊

11. Type in **7** and press **<Enter>**. Record number is **7** is displayed.

12. The postcode is incorrect. Highlight the contents of the **Post code** field and type **G53 7KP** to change it.

13. Display record **10**. Highlight the contents of the **Post code** field and press **<Delete>** to remove it.

14. Display record **12**. This school has closed. Delete this record. Check that there are now 18 records.

15. Locate the **Search** box near the **Navigation** buttons.

> Record: ◄ ◄ 12 of 18 ► ►◄ ►＊   ＜ No Filter   Search [   ]

16. Click in the **Search** box and type **Pagnall**. The record with Pagnall Street in the address is displayed.

17. Close the form <u>without</u> saving and close the database.

Driving Lesson 71 - Filtering in a Form

▣ Park and Read

An alternative to querying, filtering in a form can be useful for instant answers. There are buttons on the Ribbon to help. It is always advisable to remove a filter after use, in case the data is inadvertently saved and the unfiltered data lost.

⌒ Manoeuvres

1. Open the database **Geography**, display **All Access Objects** and open the **Country Form**.

2. Go to record **8**. Place the cursor in the **Currency** field. To filter (select) all records that have dollar as their currency, click **Selection**, [🏷 Selection ▾], in the **Sort & Filter** group on the **Home** tab and select **Equals "Dollar"**.

3. The record changes to that of Australia, the first in the table with this criteria. However, notice that the record number indicator now shows **1 of 4** with a **Filtered** indicator. The status bar also shows **Filtered**.

4. Click **Advanced**, [🗒 Advanced ▾], then select **Clear All Filters** to remove all filter definitions and include all records.

5. Click **Advanced**, [🗒 Advanced ▾], then select **Filter By Form** to set up a filter which can use two or more criteria.

```
┌─────────────────────────────────────────────┐
│ ▣  Country: Filter by Form                   │
├─────────────────────────────────────────────┤
│ ▶  Country    [                          ▼ ] │
│    Region     [                          ]   │
│    Capital    [                          ]   │
│    Population [                          ]   │
│    Area       [                          ]   │
│    Density    [                          ]   │
│    Currency   [                          ]   │
│    Language   [                          ]   │
└─────────────────────────────────────────────┘
```

6. In the **Language** field enter **English** and in the **Density** field enter **>10**.

7. Click **Advanced**, then **Apply Filter/Sort**. There are **4** records. Scroll through them to establish that the criteria have been met.

8. Clear all filters as described above and leave the form open for the next Driving Lesson.

Driving Lesson 72 - Printing from a Form

▣ Park and Read

A form is designed to be viewed on screen, but there will be occasions when a hard copy is required. Once a form has been previewed, then all records or specific records/pages of records can be printed.

⟨⟩ Manoeuvres

1.   The **Country Form** should still be open from the previous Driving Lesson.

2.   Click the **Office** button and move the cursor over **Print** to display printing options.

ⓘ *Selecting **Quick Print** from the options will send the whole form to the default printer with no further intervention.*

3.   Select **Print Preview** from the options. Buttons on the **Ribbon** can set the orientation of the print to **Landscape** or **Portrait** Make sure it is set to **Portrait**. The form properties have been designed so that several records can be displayed on a page, but no record is split over two pages. The records will be spread over ten pages, but this may vary if the margin settings have been changed.

4.   Click the **Print** button to display the **Print** dialog box.

5.   To print only one specific page, click on **Pages** in the **Print Range**. In the **From** and **To** boxes type in **10**.

```
┌─ Print Range ─────────────────────────────┐
│  ○ All                                     │
│                                            │
│  ◉ Pages  From:    10  To:     10          │
│                                            │
│  ○ Selected Record(s)                      │
└────────────────────────────────────────────┘
```

6.   Click **OK**. Only the tenth page will be printed. Close **Print Preview**.

7.   Go to the first record and right click in the **Region** field (**Asia**). Select **Equals "Asia"** from the shortcut menu. Six records are selected.

8.   Click in the **Population** field and click the **Descending** sort button, [Z↓A], on the **Home** tab to sort the forms into descending order of population.

9.   Click the **Office** button and click **Print**. The **Print** dialog box is displayed.

10.   Leave the **Print Range** as **All** and click **OK**. Only the six filtered records will be printed. They will be printed in the sorted order.

11.   Clear all filters, close the form <u>without</u> saving and close the database.

Driving Lesson 73 - Deleting a Form

▣ Park and Read

Once a form is no longer required, or if it is not working out as expected during design, then it can be deleted.

↱ Manoeuvres

1.   Open the database **Daley** and display **All Access Objects**.

2.   There are two forms available, neither is required. Click on **Cars** but do not open it.

3.   From the **Home** tab, click the **Delete** button, ✕ Delete ▾.

> **Microsoft Office Access**
>
> ⚠ **Do you want to permanently delete the form 'Cars'?**
>
> If you click Yes, you won't be able to undo the deletion.
>
> [Yes]   [No]

4.   Select **Yes** at the prompt. The **Cars** form is deleted.

5.   There is another way to delete objects. Right click on **Jobs subform**.

6.   Select **Delete** from the shortcut menu.

7.   Select **Yes** at the prompt. The **Jobs subform** form is deleted.

8.   Close the database.

Driving Lesson 74 - Revision

This Driving Lesson covers the features introduced in this section. Try not to refer to the preceding Driving Lessons while completing it.

1. Use the **Form** button, [Form], to create a quick new form for the table **Houses** from the **Houses** database.

2. Change the form title to **Current Houses**.

3. Format the title text as **Arial**, **24pt**, **Bold**. Reduce the **Label** box to just fit the title and reduce the **Form Header** size to fit the label, if necessary.

> *In Layout View it does this automatically.*

4. Increase the size of the **Form Footer** to about 1cm and add a label with your name containing your name.

5. Save the form as **Houses Form** and switch to **Form View**.

6. Filter by selection all the records that include the word **House** in their **Type** field (use the **contains "House"** option). **Print Preview** the result.

7. Sort these records into ascending order by **Town**.

8. Print out only the last page. Remove all filters and sorts.

9. Close the form and database.

10. Open the database **Mailing**.

11. Use the wizard to create a new, **Columnar** form showing all fields from the **Mailing** table. Call the form **School Mail**.

12. Filter all the **school** records and **Print Preview** them.

13. Print only pages 2 and 3 from this filter.

14. Close this form and database <u>without</u> saving.

> *Answers to this exercise can be found at the end of this guide.*

If you experienced any difficulty completing the Revision, refer back to the Driving Lessons in this section, then re-do the revision.

Driving Lesson 75 - Revision

This Driving Lesson covers the features introduced in this section. Try not to refer to the preceding Driving Lessons while completing it.

1. Open the **Geography** database.

2. Create a query based on the **Country** table including the following fields: **Country**, **Region**, **Capital**, **Population** and **Area**.

3. Add criteria to select populations over 50 million.

4. Save the query as **Over 50**.

5. Create a form using the **Form Wizard** based on this query.

6. Place all the fields from the query on the form.

7. Make it **Columnar** and choose a suitable style.

8. Name the form **Over 50**.

9. Change the title in the **Form Header** to **Densely Populated Countries**. Resize the title label and header area.

10. Change all of the text in the **Detail** area of the form to **Book Antiqua** size **12**.

11. Check that all the data is displayed, if not resize the fields using the handles so that no data is truncated.

12. Sort the records by **Area** ascending.

13. Add a label in the **Form Footer** and enter your name.

14. Preview the data. Print out all of the records.

15. Close the database, saving the changes to the form.

If you experienced any difficulty completing the Revision, refer back to the Driving Lessons in this section, then re-do the revision.

Once you are confident with the features, complete the Record of Achievement Matrix referring to the section at the end of the guide. Only when competent move on to the next Section.

Section 8
Reports & Exporting
Data

By the end of this Section you should be able to:

Create a Quick Report

Modify and Delete Reports

Preview and Print Report

Sort Data in a Report

Group Data in Reports

Perform Calculations in Reports

Export Data to Various Formats

To gain an understanding of the above features, work through the **Driving Lessons** in this **Section**.

For each **Driving Lesson**, read the **Park and Read** instructions, without touching the keyboard, then work through the numbered steps of the **Manoeuvres** on the computer. Complete the **Revision Exercise(s)** at the end of the section to test your knowledge.

Driving Lesson 76 - Quick Report

Park and Read

A report is usually used to present selected information from a table or query in printed format. Calculations can be performed and data can be presented in a variety of ways. A quick simple report can be produced by *Access* with virtually no user involvement.

Manoeuvres

1.   Open the database **Cia** and select but do not open, the **Products** table.

2.   Select the **Create** tab on the **Ribbon**, then click the **Report** button. A quick report is created based on all the fields and records from the selected table, **Products**.

Reports, like forms, can be based on any table or any query.

3.   The report is shown in **Layout View** by default with the **Format** tab displayed. Click the drop down arrow on the **View** button and select **Print Preview** to show the report as it will print out. The magnifier ^{Q} can be used to zoom in and out of the view.

4.   To save the report for future use, first close the **Print Preview** view, then right click on the **object** tab for the report and select **Save**.

*Alternatively, click the **Office Button** and select **Save As**.*

5.   Because this report was generated automatically, *Access* suggests the name **Products**, the same name as the table.

6.   Change the name to **Product List** and click **OK**. Close the database.

7.   Open the database **Daley**.

8.   To create a report based on a query, select the **Owners** query, select the **Create** tab on the **Ribbon**, then click the **Report** button.

9.   The report is displayed. There are only five records because of the selection criteria in the query.

10.   After previewing the report, save it as **Previous Owners** and close it, then close the database.

Driving Lesson 77 - Grouped Report: Wizard

🅿 Park and Read

It is possible to create reports with more control over the output, including grouping data in a report, so that records containing the same information, in a particular field, can appear grouped together. The wizard helps in this process, by asking step by step questions.

𝄐 Manoeuvres

1. Open the **Houses** database.

2. Select the **Create** tab and click on **Report Wizard**, 🔍 Report Wizard.

3. The first dialog box of the **Report Wizard** is displayed. Make sure the **Houses** table is selected as the source of data (**Table/Queries**). Select from the drop down list if necessary.

4. Click ⟩⟩ to place all of the available fields on the report. A choice of individual fields could be made using ⟩ instead if required. By selecting fields individually in a different order they can be made to appear on the report in that order.

> **Report Wizard**
>
> Which fields do you want on your report?
>
> You can choose from more than one table or query.
>
> Tables/Queries
> Table: Houses ▾
>
> Available Fields: Selected Fields:
>
>   ⟩   Bedrooms
>   ⟩⟩   Garage
>   Garden
>   Heating
>   Glazed
>   ⟨   Comment
>   ⟨⟨   Offers
>   Status
>
> Cancel   < Back   Next >   Finish

5. Select the **Comment** field and click ⟨ to remove the field from the selection. Remove **Status** in the same way.

6. Click **Next**. If no grouping is selected, the report will be a simple listing of records. This report will group together all records for the same **Town**. Select the **Town** field and click on **>** to create the grouping.

Driving Lesson 77 - Continued

7.   Click **Next**. Sort alphabetically (**Ascending**) by **Type**,

i   *Clicking the* [Ascending] *button would reverse the sort order to **Descending**.*

8.   Click the **Summary Options** button.

9.   Various calculation options are shown for any numeric fields on the report. Click in **Avg**, **Min** and **Max** for the **Price** field.

Driving Lesson 77 - Continued

10. Click **OK** and then **Next**. Choose the **Stepped Layout** and **Landscape Orientation**.

11. Click **Next**. Choose the **Civic** style on the next screen and click **Next**.

12. Finally, name the report **Grouped Town**.

13. Click **Finish**. The report is saved and displayed in **Print Preview**. The wizard is not always perfect, some fields may not be big enough and will need enlarging. Adjustments to field sizes and positions are described in the next exercise. The generated report can be too wide for a single page, if so, make sure that **Narrow Margins** and a **Size** of **A4** are selected.

14. The properties are all grouped by **Town** and appear in **Type** order within that town. Summaries are shown for each group.

15. Close the report and close the database.

Driving Lesson 78 - Modifying a Report

▣ Park and Read

Any report can be modified after it has been created. A report produced by the wizard, for example, may not display the data in exactly the way required.

Any area of a report can be altered, edited or formatted in **Layout View** or **Design View**. **Layout** view allows changes to the report format whilst the actual data is being displayed which is useful when setting field sizes for example. **Design** view shows only the field definitions but allows a greater range of changes to be made.

⌒ Manoeuvres

1. Open the **Staff** database and create a query based on the **Staff** and the **Courses** tables. Include **Title, Surname, First Name** from **Staff** and **Date** and **Course** from **Courses**.

2. In the **Date** criteria include only those dates in the 1990's,
       >=1/1/90 and <=31/12/99

3. Save the query as **Completed Courses** and close it.

4. Select the **Create** tab and click **Report Wizard**.

5. Select the **Completed Courses** query as the source and add all of the fields to the report. On the next screen leave the suggestion for viewing the data as it is.

6. Choose to **Group** by **Surname** and sort by **Date** in ascending order. Leave the layout and style as suggested.

7. Change the report title to **Courses in the 1990s** and click **Finish**. The report will be saved and displayed in **Print Preview**.

8. Close **Print Preview** and switch to **Layout View** to view the design of the report. The **Title** and **First Name** are a little far apart. Click in the **Title** field for the first record. The **Title** field is far too large for the data.

9. Click and drag the right edge of the first **Title** field to the left to reduce the field size.

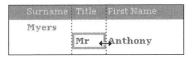

> ℹ *Always check that the field remains large enough to display any possible data and labels.*

☞

Driving Lesson 78 - Continued

10. Release the mouse button to set the field size. Other fields and their labels are automatically moved to the left to maintain the overall layout.

11. Click in any **Date** field and click **Align Text Left** from the **Font** group. Repeat this for the **Date** column heading. Enlarge the field if necessary.

12. Change to **Design View**. Notice that the wizard has created a **Report Header** (containing the report title), a **Page Header** (containing column headings), a **Page Footer** (containing the date and page numbers) and a **Report Footer** (currently empty).

i *In a report where these areas are not present they can be added by selecting buttons in the Show/Hide group on the Arrange tab.*

13. Select the **Title** field in the **Page Header** area. Press **<Delete>**. Notice *Access* also removes the **Title** heading from the **Page Header** and moves other fields to close up the gap.

14. This automatic formatting is because the fields on the report are included in a **Control Layout**. This can be very useful but prevents individual fields being moved in isolation. Try and move the **Course** field to the right of the page. It is not allowed.

15. With the **Course** field still selected, display the **Arrange** tab and click **Remove** from the **Control Layout** group.

16. Now drag the courses field about **4cms** to the right. Because it is no longer in a **Control Layout** it will move. For the same reason the **Course** heading will have to be dragged and aligned separately.

17. Click in the **Report Header** and change the title to **1990 Courses**.

18. Click the lower edge of the **Report Footer** bar and drag it down to create a data area about **2cm** deep. Use the button in the **Controls** group of the **Design** tab to create a **Label** box in this area and add the text **Created by** and then your name.

19. Preview the report to see the new features, then save the report, close it, and close the database.

i *The manipulation of fields in a Report and a Form is exactly the same.*

Driving Lesson 79 - Other Calculations in Reports

P Park and Read

While many calculations can be carried out during the report wizard, others can be added to the report after the wizard is complete. This involves adding a text box to contain the calculation. The positioning of the box is all-important, especially in a grouped report.

All calculation definitions begin with an equals sign, **=**, and all field names used are contained in square brackets, **[ ]**. Calculations can use existing functions like **Count** and **Sum** or mathematical operators, e.g. **=[Hours] * [Rate]**.

Manoeuvres

1.   Open the **Houses** database and the **Grouped Town** report.

2.   Switch to **Design View**. The wizard has created a group header (**Town Header**) and a group footer (**Town Footer**). To count the number of properties in each town, a calculation must be added to the group footer.

3.   Select the text box in the **Town Footer** that begins **Summary for...** and delete it.

4.   Increase the size of the footer and from the **Design** tab click the **Text Box** button,[abl]. Draw a text box in the left side of the **Town Footer**. This immediately becomes two boxes, a label and an unbound box. Enter the following information in the label and the unbound box.

No of properties | =Count([Address])

---

i *If the boxes overlap, move them apart. Usually moving a field or label moves the other object as well. Move individual objects by dragging the black handle at their top left corner.*

i *Every record with content in the Address field will be counted.*

5.   Add another text box below the first and enter the following data

Sum of properties | =Sum([Price])

. Make the **Town Footer** deeper, if necessary.

6.   **Print Preview** the report. Because the calculations were placed in the **Town Footer**, each town now shows the number of properties and the total price of the properties in that town.

7.   Enlarge fields where necessary to improve the look of the report, then save the report and leave it open for the next Driving Lesson.

Driving Lesson 80 - Printing from a Report

⊞ Park and Read

By default, once the design of a report is completed, the view becomes **Preview**. This allows the creator to view how the report will print and whether all fields will be displayed. If they are not, then the formatting and editing will have to be done in **Layout** or **Design** view.

Once satisfied with the layout, you can print the report. It is possible to print all of a report or to specify pages.

⟨⟩ Manoeuvres

1.   The **Houses** database and the **Grouped Town** report will be open from the previous Driving Lesson.

2.   Make sure the report is displayed in **Print Preview**. Use the **View** drop down button if necessary.

3.   The report covers approximately six pages (depending on how big the footer area was made). Click the navigation buttons to confirm this, then click the **Page Setup** button.

4.   The **Margins** tab allows the white space around the report to be altered, note that it is in millimetres. The values shown here are for the **Narrow Margins** setting. Change all margins to **15mm** and click **OK**.

ℹ️ *Changing margins or having the wrong paper size set can change the number of printed pages. It can also cause forms to overflow horizontally, doubling the number of pages in the print, some of which may be almost blank.*

Driving Lesson 80 - Continued

5.   Click the **Page Setup** button and click the **Page** tab.

6.   There are several paper and envelope sizes available from here, as well as the orientation options. The actual options available will depend on the type of printer that is connected. Select **Letter**, from the **Size** drop down list if available and change the orientation to **Portrait**.

ℹ️   *Paper Size* *may already be set to* *Letter*.

Page Setup
Print Options   **Page**   Columns
Orientation
[A] ● Portrait   [A] ○ Landscape
Paper
Size: Letter
Source: Automatically Select
Printer for Grouped Town
● Default Printer
○ Use Specific Printer   Printer...
OK   Cancel

7.   Click the **Columns** tab. These settings control the number of columns in a multiple column report, e.g. when printing address labels, they may be printed 3 across a page. This will not concern you in this module.

8.   Click **OK** to view the newly formatted report. It now covers more pages and does not look very good. Change the orientation back to **Landscape**, the paper size to **A4**, and all margins to **6mm**.

ℹ️   *Paper Size, Orientation* *and* *Margins* *can all be set using buttons on the* *Ribbon. These buttons work in exactly the same way when printing tables forms and queries.*

9.   Click the **Margins** button on the **Ribbon** and select **Narrow**.

10. Click the **Print** button on the **Ribbon** to display the **Print** dialog box.

Driving Lesson 80 - Continued

11. In the **Print Range** area select to print only page **2** (enter 2 in the **From** and **To** box). Click **OK** to print.

12. Select **Page Setup, Print Options** tab, and change all the margins to **20mm**. Click in the **Print Data Only** box and click **OK** to view the effect – no headers or field names are shown.

13. Alter the **Top** and **Bottom** margins to **30mm**. Remove the check from **Print Data Only** to reinstate the report headers and footers. Click **OK** to view the result.

14. Click the **Margins** button on the **Ribbon** and select **Narrow**.

15. Click **Print** to view the **Print** dialog box. To print only specific pages from a report, enter the start and finish number in the **From** and **To** boxes. Enter data to print from pages **2** to **5**.

16. Click **OK** to send the selected pages to the printer, or **Cancel** to cancel the print and save paper.

17. To print a complete report, redisplay the **Print** dialog box and select **All** from the **Print Range** settings. Click **OK** to print the report, or **Cancel** to cancel the print and save paper.

18. Close the report and the database <u>without</u> saving any changes.

i   *Right click on a report in the **Navigation** pane and select **Print** from the shortcut menu to send all pages immediately to the default printer.*

Driving Lesson 81 - Deleting a Report

Park and Read

As with all other database objects, once a report becomes obsolete it can be deleted.

Manoeuvres

1. Open the **Staff** database make sure **All Access Objects** are displayed in the navigation pane.

2. The report **Courses in the 1990's** was short term and is no longer required.

3. Click on it, but do not open it.

4. Click the **Delete** button, ❌ Delete ▾ , from the **Home** tab.

ℹ *Alternatively, right click on the report in the **Navigation** pane and select **Delete** from the shortcut menu.*

> **Microsoft Office Access**   ✕
>
> ⚠ **Do you want to permanently delete the report 'Courses in the 1990s'?**
>
> If you click Yes, you won't be able to undo the deletion.
>
>   Yes   No

5. At the dialog box, select **Yes** to permanently delete the report.

6. Close the database.

Driving Lesson 82 - Exporting Data

🅿 Park and Read

You have seen how reports can be used to provide a printed copy of information selected from a table or query. Other forms of output can be obtained from a database by exporting data. A table or query can be exported in spreadsheet, text or XML format (for viewing on the web) and then saved for future use. The data can then be used in different software packages.

👉 Manoeuvres

1. Open the **Cia** database and open the **Customer Details** table, which is to be exported as a spreadsheet file.

2. Select the **External Data** tab on the **Ribbon** and click the **Excel** button from the **Export** group.

```
Export - Excel Spreadsheet                                              ? ×

    Select the destination for the data you want to export

    Specify the destination file name and format.

    File name:   C:\Users\Brian\Documents\Customer Details.xlsx          Browse...

    File format:  Excel Workbook (*.xlsx)        ▾

    Specify export options.

      ☐ Export data with formatting and layout.
        Select this option to preserve most formatting and layout information when exporting a table, query, form, or report.
```

3. Click the **Browse** button to open the **File Save** dialog box. Use this to set the location for the exported file to the supplied data folder.

4. Change the name of the file at the end of the **File name** path to **Customers** and click **Save**.

5. In the **Export** dialog box, check **Export data with formatting and layout** and click **OK**. The data is exported.

6. Click **Close** at the next screen then close the **Customer Details** table.

7. Tables can be exported without opening them. Select, but do not open, the **Products** table, which is to be exported as a text file. Click the **Text File** button in the **Export** group of the **External Data** tab. This process will export both text and .csv files.

8. The file path should already be to the supplied data folder (from the previous export). Change the name of the file to **Product file**. Make sure none of the export options are selected and click **OK**.

👉

Driving Lesson 82 - Continued

9. From the **Export Text Wizard** select **Delimited**.

10. Click **Next** and select **Comma** as the delimiter and **"** as the **Text Qualifier**. Click **Next** and then **Finish**. Click **Close** at the final screen.

11. Now open the **Orders** table, which is to be exported in **XML** file format.

12. From the **Export** group of the **External Data** tab, click the **More** button and choose **XML File** from the list.

[i] *Data can be exported in several formats from this list.*

13. Name the file **Orderinfo** and click **OK**.

14. From the **Export XML** dialog box, ensure **Data (XML)** and **Schema of the data** are selected.

15. Click **OK**, then click **Close** in the **Export** dialog box..

16. Output from queries can be exported in exactly the same way. Create a query in **Design View** based on the **Suppliers** table which lists **Supplier Name** and **Supplier Phone**. Save the query as **Phone List**.

17. Click the **Excel** button from the **Export** group on the **External Data** tab export the data as **Phone List** (queries can be exported in all the same formats as tables).

18. Check the **formatting** box and click **OK**. Click **Close** then close the query.

19. To see the various files that have been exported, open the **Documents** folder from the **Start** menu.

20. Locate and select the data folder to see its contents. The exported files are all present.

21. Open the files **Customers.xlsx** and **Phone List.xlsx** in *Excel* and **Product file.txt** in *Word* or *Notepad* to see how they have been stored. Open **Orderinfo.xml** to see its format.

22. Close all open applications including the **Cia** database.

Driving Lesson 83 - Revision

This Driving Lesson covers the features introduced in this section. Try not to refer to the preceding Driving Lessons while completing it.

1.   Open the database **Geography**.

2.   Create a quick report for the **Regions** table. Save the report as **Regional**. How many pages does it have?

3.   Print out the first 2 pages.

4.   In **Design View**, change the format of <u>all</u> fields to **Britannic Bold**.

5.   Change all text to **12pt** except the title font which should be **24pt**. Check that all the data is still displayed fully.

6.   Close the report saving any changes.

7.   Export the **Country** table in **Excel Workbook (*.xlsx)** format, as **List**. Save a formatted version of the data.

8.   Close the **Geography** database and open the database **Mailing**.

9.   Create a report based on the **Mailing** table, using the **Report Wizard**.

10. Select all of the fields for the report, but do not add grouping levels.

11. Sort by **Name** in descending order.

12. Make the layout **Columnar** and the orientation **Portrait**.

13. Select the **Office** style and name the report **Contacts**.

14. Change all the margins to **6mm**.

15. Print the first page of the report, then close the report saving any changes and close the database.

ⓘ *Answers to this exercise can be found at the end of this guide.*

If you experienced any difficulty completing the Revision, refer back to the Driving Lessons in this section, then re-do the revision.

Driving Lesson 84 - Revision

This Driving Lesson covers the features introduced in this section. Try not to refer to the preceding Driving Lessons while completing it.

1. Open the database **Football Agent** and create a query based on **Current Status** and **Past Clubs** tables.

2. Include the fields **Surname, First Name, Date Joined, Current Club, Past Clubs** and **Transfer fee**. Save the query as **Commission**.

3. Use **Report Wizard** to create a report based on this query. Place all available fields on the report, and group by **Surname**.

4. Sort by **Date Joined** and select to show the average transfer fee.

5. Choose the **Stepped** layout and **Landscape** orientation. Choose any style, change the name of the report to **Commission** and click **Finish**.

6. When the report is viewed make sure page size is set to **A4**.

7. Switch to **Layout View** and make sure all data is fully and clearly displayed and correctly aligned.

8. To calculate the commission on each transfer, add a **Text Box** at the right of the **Detail** area.

9. Delete the **Label** for the new field and add a new **Label** in the **Page Header** area above the new unbound field. Type the text **Commission** into the label and make sure it has the same formatting as other labels.

10. Type **=[Transfer Fee]*10/100** in the new unbound field. This will give a result of 10% of the transfer fee.

11. Save this report then switch to **Report View** to view the calculations.

12. Draw a text box in the **Report Footer** area with a label, of **Total Commission**, and a formula of **=Sum([Transfer Fee]*10/100)**.

13. Make any other formatting changes required to enhance the appearance of the report and print the result. Save the report and close it.

14. Close *Access*.

If you experienced any difficulty completing the Revision, refer back to the Driving Lessons in this section, then re-do the revision.

Once you are confident with the features, complete the Record of Achievement Matrix referring to the section at the end of the guide.

Answers

Driving Lesson 8

Step 3   6 tables

Step 9   The **Design** tab

Driving Lesson 9

Step 2   4 objects

Step 3   The **Database Tools** tab

Step 4   The **Home** tab

Step 7   8 results, if connected to Office Online (6 results if Offline)

Driving Lesson 34

Step 8   Record 5

Step 9   Record 8

Driving Lesson 35

Step 11 Argentina, Brazil, Canada, Mexico, Peru and USA

Step 13 Finland, Libya, Israel and Norway

Driving Lesson 41

Step 8   There are **7** countries in the Middle East region.

Step 9   There are **9** capital cities beginning with B.

Driving Lesson 43

Step 2   There are **3** customers living in County Durham.

Step 7   There are **7** houses with **carpets** in the **Comments**

Driving Lesson 48

Step 2   There are **4** properties in Whitehaven.

Step 3   **13** properties have 3 bedrooms.

Step 4   There are **6** properties in a Town beginning with C.

Step 5   There are **3** flats.

Step 8   There are **47** countries on the database.

Step 9   **6** countries have English as their main language.

Step 10 **Ethiopia** is first

Step 11 There are **26** non-European countries.

Step 12 **Japan** is the most densely populated country outside Europe.

Driving Lesson 49

Step 3   There are **4** records with **Mr** as the **Title**.

Step 7   There are **6** unpaid orders.

Step 12 Yes the **Saab**, registration **E476 WSG**

Step 13 Because the data type is not number

Driving Lesson 50

Step 8   There are **4**.

Step 9   There are **3** men involved in sales.

Step 10 **3** employees started work in 1985.

Step 11 Only **1** person is paid £15,000.

Step 12 The oldest member of staff is **Ian Chapman** (unless you have added someone older).

Driving Lesson 63

Step 4   There are **5** properties in Cockermouth.

Step 6   There are **11** properties with a garage.

Step 7   There are **26** properties for sale

Step 8   There are **13** properties with three bedrooms.

Step 9   There are **4** properties in Whitehaven.

Step 10 There are **8** properties costing less than £22,000.

Step 11 There are **3** properties costing between 40 and 50 thousand.

Step 12 **Whitehaven, 9 Deepdene, Listed Building**.

Step 13 **11** properties have offers on them.

Driving Lesson 64

Step 1   **4** players earn more than £100,000

Step 7   **7** repairs carried out on 02/01/02

Step 12 There are **3** different staff.

Step 13 **3** staff have been on an introductory course.

Step 14 **Mr Waldram (Valdron)**.

Driving Lesson 74

Step 6   There are **18** houses.

Step 12 There are **12** schools.

Driving Lesson 83

Step 2   The report has **4** pages.

Glossary

AND	A logical operator. Can be used in queries when a value must satisfy all of the conditions.
Field	The separate areas in a table, which form Rows and Columns and Records.
Foreign Key	A primary key from table A, which is also used as a key field in table B is called a Foreign Key.
Form	A user defined display on the screen which controls how the user interacts with the database.
Integer	A positive or negative whole number (no decimals) or zero.
Long Integer	A larger positive or negative whole number, or zero.
Macro	An automated way of performing one or a series of actions.
One-to-many	Any one record from table A may be related to one or many records from table B.
One-to-one	One record from table A is related to one record from table B.
OR	A logical operator. Can be used in queries when a value needs to match at least one of two or more conditions.
Primary Key	A field which uniquely identifies a record, e.g. telephone number in a table.
Query	A method of extracting specific information from a database.
Quick Report	A report automatically generated by *Access*.
QuickForm	A form created automatically by *Access*.
Record	A set of inter-related data.
Referential Integrity	When applied to a relationship, data cannot be altered or deleted in the second table, without the primary table first being altered. This ensures the data in the tables is always valid.
Relationships	The ability to connect tables of data, so that no data need to be repeated.
Report	A hard copy of related data taken from a database.
Table	A form of data storage consisting of Rows and Columns.
Validation Rules	Defines the permitted entry into a field which the user can make. Entries that do not conform to the rule cannot be entered.
Wildcard	Characters used in searches or queries that allow one or many letters to be replaced by the wildcard (? and *).

Index

Adding
Fields 47
Records 69

Access
Close 19
Start 10

And Queries 95

Calculated Fields 123

Closing
Access 19
Databases 19
Tables 19

Column Width
Changing 62

Create
New Database 27
New Form 102, 104
New Report 117, 118
Table Structure 29

Databases 8
Closing 19
Creating a New Database 27
Forms 100
Navigation Pane 15
Opening 13
Principles 9
Queries 82
Reports 116

Deleting
Forms 113
Queries 97
Records 57, 69
Reports 127
Tables 48

Editing
Adding Records 69
Changing the Column Width 62
Deleting Records 57
Editing a Form 108
Editing Data 66, 68
Finding Data 63
Shortcuts 70
Undo 67
Updating Records 57
Using Wildcards 64

Entering Data in a Table 34

Exporting Data 128

Field
Add New 47
Editing 39
Properties 32

Filtering 74
By Form 77
Quick Filters 78
Using Filters 76

Finding Data 63

Format
Changing Column Width 62
Field Property 32

Forms 100
Deleting 113
Describing 101
Designing a Form 106
Editing a Form 108
Editing Data 109
Filtering 111
Printing 112
Quick Forms 102
Sorting Data 109
Wizard 104

Grouped Report: Wizard 118

Help 11

Indexes 36
Duplicates 38

Moving
Using the Keyboard 25
Using the Mouse 23

Navigation Pane 15

Non-Matches 94

Online Help 11

Open
Application 10
Existing Database 13

Or Queries 96

Preview Table 43

Primary Key
Defining 35

Printing
Forms 112
Reports 124

Tables 43, 45

Queries 82
And Queries 95
Deleting 97
Editing 91
Non-Matches 94
Or Queries 96
Printing 88
Querying a Table 83
Ranges of Values 92
Related Tables 89
Saving 87
Sorting 86

Querying A Table 83

Quick Access Toolbar 10, 67

Ranges of Values 92

Records
Adding 69
Deleting 57, 69
Updating 57

Referential Integrity 56

Relationships 52
Applying 54
Referential Integrity 56

Reports 116
Quick Report 117
Calculations in 123
Deleting 127
Grouped Report Wizard 118
Modifying a Report 121
Printing 124

Revisions
Databases 20 - 21
Editing 71-73
Forms 114-115
Queries 98-99
Relationships 59-60
Reports 130-131
Sorting and Filtering 79-81
Tables 49 - 50

Ribbon 17

Searches
For Data 63
Non Matches 94

Sorting 75
Data 76
In Forms 109

Queries 86

Tables 22
Closing 19
Creating a Table Structure 29
Defining a Primary Key 35
Deleting 48
Entering Data 34
Format Field Property 32
Indexes 36
Querying a Table 83
Relationships 52
Using the Keyboard to Move 25
Using the Mouse to Move 23

Undo 67

Validation
Rules 41
Text 41

Wildcards 64

Record of Achievement Matrix

This Matrix is to be used to measure your progress while working through the guide. This is a learning reinforcement process, you judge when you are competent.

Tick boxes are provided for each feature. 1 is for no knowledge, 2 some knowledge and 3 is for competent. A section is only complete when column 3 is completed for all parts of the section.

For details on sitting ECDL Examinations in your country please contact the local ECDL Licensee or visit the European Computer Driving Licence Foundation Limited web site at http://www.ecdl.org.

Tick the Relevant Boxes **1**: No Knowledge   **2**: Some Knowledge   **3**: Competent

Section	No	Driving Lesson	1	2	3
1 Databases	1	Database Principles			
	2	Starting Access			
	3	Help			
	4	Opening an Existing Database			
	5	The Navigation Pane			
	6	The Ribbon			
	7	Closing Tables, Databases and Access			
2 Tables	10	Moving Using the Mouse			
	11	Moving Using the Keyboard			
	12	Creating a New Database - Designing & Planning			
	13	Creating a Table Structure			
	14	Format Field Property			
	15	Entering Data in a Table			
	16	Defining a Primary Key			
	17	Indexes			
	18	Duplicates			
	19	Editing Field Properties			
	20	Validation Rules/Text			
	21	Previewing and Printing a Table			
	22	Printing From a Table			
	23	Adding a New Field to an Existing Table			
	24	Deleting a Table			
3 Table Relationships	27	Table Relationships			
	28	Applying Relationships			
	29	Referential Integrity			
	30	Updating and Deleting Records			
4 Editing	33	Changing Column Width			
	34	Finding Specific Data			
	35	Using Wildcards			
	36	Editing Data			
	37	Undo			
	38	Further Editing			
	39	Adding/Deleting Records			
	40	Editing Shortcuts			

Tick the Relevant Boxes **1**: No Knowledge   **2**: Some Knowledge   **3**: Competent

Section	No	Driving Lesson	1	2	3
5 Sorting and Filtering	44	Sorting Data			
	45	Using Filters			
	46	Filters by Form			
	47	Quick Filters			
6 Queries	51	Querying a Table			
	52	Selecting in Queries			
	53	Sorting Query Results			
	54	Saving Query Results			
	55	Printing Query Results			
	56	Querying Related Tables			
	57	Editing Queries			
	58	Ranges of Values and Wildcards			
	59	Non-Matches			
	60	And Queries			
	61	Or Queries			
	62	Deleting a Query			
7 Forms	65	Forms			
	66	Quick Forms			
	67	Form Wizard			
	68	Designing a Form			
	69	Editing Form Design			
	70	Sorting and Editing Data			
	71	Filtering in a Form			
	72	Printing from a Form			
	73	Deleting a Form			
8 Reports	76	Quick Report			
	77	Grouped Report Wizard			
	78	Modifying a Report			
	79	Other Calculations in Reports			
	80	Printing from a Report			
	81	Deleting a Report			
	82	Exporting Data			

Other Products from CiA Training Ltd

CiA Training Ltd is a leading publishing company, which has consistently delivered the highest quality products since 1985. A wide range of flexible and easy to use self teach resources has been developed by CiA's experienced publishing team to aid the learning process. These include the following ECDL Foundation approved products at the time of publication of this product:

- **ECDL/ICDL Syllabus 5.0**

- **ECDL/ICDL Advanced Syllabus 2.0**

- **ECDL/ICDL Revision Series**

- **ECDL/ICDL Advanced Syllabus 2.0 Revision Series**

- **e-Citizen**

Previous syllabus versions also available - contact us for further details.

We hope you have enjoyed using our materials and would love to hear your opinions about them. If you'd like to give us some feedback, please go to:

www.ciatraining.co.uk/feedback.php

and let us know what you think.

New products are constantly being developed. For up to the minute information on our products, to view our full range, to find out more, or to be added to our mailing list, visit:

www.ciatraining.co.uk